Discharged from Mental Hospitals

Philip Bean and Patricia Mounser

MACMILLAN

in association
with

MIND
PUBLICATIONS

First published 1993 by
THE MACMILLAN PRESS LTD
Houndmills, Basingstoke, Hampshire RG21 2XS
and London
Companies and representatives
throughout the world

ISBN 0–333–44787–5 hardcover
ISBN 0–333–44788–3 paperback

A catalogue record for this book is available
from the British Library.

Printed in Hong Kong

Reprinted 1993

Series Standing Order (Issues in Mental Health)

If you would like to receive future titles in this series as they are published, you can
make use of our standing order facility. To place a standing order please contact your
bookseller or, in case of difficulty,write to us at the address below with your name
and address and the name of the series. Please state with which title you wish to
begin your standing order. (If you live outside the United Kingdom we may not have
the rights for your area, in which case we will forward your order to the publisher
concerned.)

Customer Services Department, Macmillan Distribution Ltd
Houndmills, Basingstoke, Hampshire RG21 2XS, England

Issues in Mental Health
Series Editor: Jo Campling

The care and status of persons with mental health problems has been identified as one of the key issues in health and society in the 1990s.

This series of books has been commissioned to give a multi-disciplinary perspective: legal, medical, psychiatric and social work aspects of mental health will be covered. There is also an international perspective: wherever possible, books will compare developments in a range of different countries.

PUBLISHED

Philip Bean and Patricia Mounser
Discharged from Mental Hospitals

Suman Fernando
Mental Health, Race and Culture

Shulamit Ramon (editor)
Beyond Community Care: Normalisation and Integration Work

Anne Rogers, David Pilgrim and Ron Lacey
Experiencing Psychiatry: Users' Views of Services

The *Issues in Mental Health* series is published in association with

MIND (National Association for Mental Health)
22 Harley Street, London W1N 2ED (071–6370741)

MIND is the leading mental health organisation in England and
Wales. It works for a better life for people diagnosed, labelled
or treated as mentally ill. It does this through campaigning,
influencing government policy, training, education and service
provision. Throughout its work MIND reflects its awareness of
black and ethnic communities, and draws on the expertise of
people with direct experience as providers and users of mental
health services.

The points of view expressed in this publication do not necessarily
reflect MIND policy.

Contents

List of Tables

List of Abbreviations

BASW	British Association of Social Workers
BMJ	*British Medical Journal*
CCO	Community Care Order
CMHC	Community Mental Health Centre
CMHRC	Community Mental Health Resource Centre
CPN(s)	Community Psychiatric Nurse(s)
CTO	Community Treatment Order
ECT	Electro-convulsive therapy
GP	General practitioner
MHAC	Mental Health Act Commission
MHRC	Mental Health Resource Centre
MHRT(s)	Mental Health Review Tribunal(s)
NAO	National Audit Office (UK)
RMO	Responsible Medical Officer
RSU(s)	Regional Secure Unit(s)
US	United States (adjective)
USA	United States of America (noun)

1

Introduction: An Overview of Patients Discharged from Mental Hospitals

In the 1970s an important debate developed about admissions to mental hospitals: what ought to be the legal procedures involved, how were decisions made about who should or should not be admitted, who should make those decisions and so on? It had many strands: there were those such as the civil libertarians who were concerned with patients' rights and liberties, there were others more concerned with access to resources, and still others concerned about the position of the mental hospital in society, its role, its function – and its disfunction also. Some of those critics have seen their arguments met by legislation such as the Mental Health Act 1983 in Britain, or similar such legislation elsewhere but others have not. And even then much of that legislation has been half-hearted. In Britain, for example, whilst provisions for consent to treatment have been introduced there is still no right of appeal prior to admission, nor is it clear what are and should be the rights of the patients' relatives in the procedure for compulsory admission. Nor indeed is it clear whether there are justifications for detaining patients at all, simply because they have mental-health problems. It must be added that new criticisms have arisen, some produced by the legislation that tried to meet earlier ones: for example, the holding power granted to nurses to prevent voluntary patients from leaving hospital (under Section 5 of the Mental Health Act 1983), seems entirely unjustified, whilst the training programme for the Approved Social Workers scheme has not proved successful (see Bean, 1986 and Goodman, 1989).

Even so, and with the introduction in Britain of the 1983 Mental Health Act, the debate settled down or, rather, shifted to another plane. If we use the British experience to illustrate the point then attention will seem to be drawn, as if naturally, to questions about what was happening inside the mental hospital: about the nature of psychiatric treatments, of consent procedures, or about the nature or essence of madness itself. Had anyone asked us to predict the next stage of interest after the Act of 1983 we would have said it was reasonable to expect discharges from mental hospitals to be the priority: who goes out and why, how decisions are made about discharges, and how the discharge procedure should be planned? (The Mental Health Act Commission had agreed that 'discharges of patients should be regarded as a process rather than an event – a process of stages leading up to the event of physical discharge. Sudden discharges should be a thing of the past': MHAC, 1985). We would have expected these questions to run parallel with those for admission if only because it was logical to expect discharges to be dealt with according to the same priority and seriousness as their counterparts. We would also have expected that there would have been interest in developing the same standards of adjudication as for admissions, because it seems logical to base discharges on the same premise and also important to discharge patients from hospital at the earliest possible opportunity. Getting out is, or should be, as important as getting in.

But this third phase has not happened. The logical progression of the debate has been interrupted and overtaken by events. Mental hospitals the world over have divested themselves of their traditional role of providing asylum for people with mental health problems. The new term is *decarceration* or *deinstitutionalisation*, where everybody gets out whether they are ready or not – or *transinstitutionalisation* where everybody gets out but goes straight to some other institution, whether an old people's home, a hostel or a prison.

Deinstitutionalisation is more than a policy, it is a social ideology. Its supporters hold that deinstitutionalisation is desirable to the extent that psychiatric patients should live independently, assume responsibility for themselves and adapt to the demands and rigours of life outside the mental hospital (Sands, 1984). In its pure form it has two elements:

(i) avoiding placing psychiatric patients in institutions;
(ii) expanding community services to enable those persons to remain in the community.

It means in fact closing the mental hospitals and replacing them with a system of community care.

It is not the intention here to evaluate decarceration, or deinstitutionalisation, or even its corollary, community care. That is being done elsewhere in this series. Rather the aim is to concentrate on the nature of discharges and being discharged; not so much to ask why people get out of mental hospitals, for every one does, but to define what is meant by a discharge. It also means asking a number of other questions:

- What effect does this policy have on other institutions?
- What links are there between community provision and the discharge movement, or indeed between community provision and the remnants of the mental hospital system.
- What does rehabilitation or the newly fashionable term, sectorisation, mean under these circumstances?
- When patients are discharged, what are their rights?
- Will those rights be removed if the Community Treatment Orders (CTOs) are introduced, as they have been in the USA or Australia and are expected to be in Canada and Israel?
- Will the patient be transferred from one institution – i.e. the mental hospital – only to be coerced and controlled elsewhere?

Above all:

- What has been the effect of deinstitutionalisation on hospital patients in other institutions such as those in the Special Hospitals (or hospitals for the criminally insane as they are called elsewhere) or prisons?

Might it be that the ease and speed of discharge from the mental hospital has made it additionally difficult to consider transfer to and out of anywhere else?

It is our opinion that these transfers from Special Hospitals or prisons are seriously threatened by the demise of mental hospitals. Being unable to promote discharges from the prison or Special Hospitals, those secure institutions must adapt and change accordingly. For the prison this may mean developing new and more expensive psychiatric treatment facilities within the prison hospital system, and for the Special Hospitals it may mean seeking new ways of providing after-care and post-discharge arrangements. The so-called 'knock-on' effect which comes from discharging everyone from the mental hospitals is bound to be extensive.

Background to the debate

The discharge of patients from mental hospitals once symbolised all that these hospitals represented. Indeed, the physical discharge of patients came to indicate the success of mental hospitals, whose purpose it was to take mentally disturbed individuals and restore them, through a process called 'moral treatment' (later to be replaced by the more scientifically-based psychiatric treatment) to the full possession of their senses. Moral treatment replaced a much harsher regime where treatment had been physical and the use of chains and straitjackets commonplace. The treatment of George III exemplifies this era when patients were no longer seen as human beings. He was treated by being encased in a machine that allowed no movement, and he was frequently starved and beaten, and subjected to menacing and violent language (Scull, 1982).

Thereafter, the philosophy that developed with the mental hospitals, then called *asylums*, projected them as the ideal therapeutic environment within which this goal of 'cure' of the individual could be achieved. Indeed, in 1868 Henry Maudsley wrote on the subject of moral treatment in asylums, and we think it is worth quoting in full as it exemplifies the philosophy of this era:

> To remove the patient from the midst of those circumstances under which insanity has been produced must be the first aim of treatment. There is always extreme difficulty in treating satisfactorily an insane person in his own house, amongst his own kindred, where he has been accustomed to exercise authority, to exact attention; and where he continually finds new occasions for outbreak of anger or fresh food for his delusions. An entire change in the surroundings will sometimes of itself lead to his recovery: if the patient is melancholic, he no longer receives the impressions of those whom having most loved when well he now mistrusts, or concerning whom he grieves that his affections are so much changed; if he is maniacal he is not specially irritated by the opposition of those to whose acquiescence he has been accustomed, nor encouraged by their submission to his whims and their indulgence of his follies (quoted in Busfield, 1986).

In keeping with this aim of 'moral treatment' the asylums of this time began to compete with each other in laying claims to cures, which were greatly belied by the turnover of their inmate populations. That is, data for the time shows a formidable rise in hospital populations, on the one hand, and estimates of 'curable' patients that the asylums contained, on the other. The relative absence of any data showing the number of discharges of those actually cured remains scarce. The metropolitan Commissioners in Lunacy, for example, reported in 1844 on asylum superintendents' estimates of the number and percentage of curable patients in asylums in England and Wales (Table 1.1) which shows a wide variety of claims to the cure of inmates.

What remains unclear is what they actually meant by curable, and whether they were saying that these patients were discharged, or could be discharged. In fact, patients were discharged from Bethlem after twelve months if not cured, sooner of course if they recovered; they were released on a month's trial leave of absence before they were discharged (Allderidge, 1979). It must be said, however, that this was the period before the mass influx of pauper inmates and also that Bethlem and St Luke's hospitals selected their patients on the basis of whether they could be cured or not. (Scull, 1979). Other figures available suggest, however, that they were referring to discharges. Table 1.2 is an example.

Clearly, this data provides an insight into the situation relating to discharges in the nineteenth century. The proportion seen to be cured (that is, no longer in need of sanctuary) is seen to fall steadily until eventually it appears that more inmates leave in coffins each year than are restored to society in full possession of their senses (Scull, 1979).

Table 1.1 *Asylum superintendents' estimates of the number and percentage of curable patients in asylums in England and Wales in 1844*

Type of asylum	Private			Pauper		
	Total	Number curable	%	Total	Number curable	%
Provincial licensed houses	1426	412	28.9	1920	637	33.2
Metropolitan licensed houses	973	153	15.7	854	111	13.0
County asylums	245	645	24.9	4244	651	15.4
Charity hospitals	536	127	23.7	343	59	17.2
Military/naval	168	18	10.7	–	–	–
Bethlem	265	181	68.5	90	no estimate	
St Luke's	177	93	52.5	31	16	51.6

Source: Metropolitan Commissioners in Lunacy, Report 1844, pp. 185, 187.

6 *Discharged from Mental Hospitals*

Table 1.2 *Cure and mortality rates in county and borough asylums, 1870–90*

Year	Number cured as percentage of total number resident	Number of deaths as percentage of total number of resident
1870	8.54	8.48
1880	3.31	7.40
1890	7.68	8.20

Source: 25th Annual Report of Commissioners in Lunacy, 1871, pp. 112–15; 35th Annual Report, 1881, pp. 148–51; 45th Annual Report, 1891, pp. 96–9.

The extraordinary reversal of this situation over the past twenty-five years has led the same reform energies who acclaimed the asylum as both curative and humane, to denounce it as 'a colossal mistake whose commission can only be redeemed by its abolition' (Scull, 1982). That is, everything that had gone before had been completely wrong, and some would argue intentionally malicious. The 'dawning of enlightenment' also revealed new ways of dealing with such grand malevolence (Allderidge, 1979). In Britain, as in America, the discharge of patients from mental hospitals has become the policy which heralds the demise of the asylum whose hegemony had lasted for over two centuries. This policy, in Britain, was first announced by Enoch Powell (then Minister of Health) in 1961 at the Annual Conference of the National Association of Mental Health. Following this announcement the 'Community Care' Blue Book was published in April 1963 purporting to offer the alternative to the defunct asylum (Jones, 1983). The proposed closure of sixty of Britain's mental hospitals by 1991 announced by the Department of Health and Social Security (DHSS) (Cohen 1988) leaves us in little doubt that Britain intends to follow America where mental patients are quickly discharged to the community. This deinstitutionalisation is what Scull calls the 'state-sponsored policy of closing down asylums, prisons, and reformatories' (quoted in Busfield, 1986) and has led some critics to argue that it represents an 'enlightened revolution or an abdication of responsibility' (Bassuk and Gerson, 1978). Yet others have shown that changes of this magnitude are not new, but tend to have cyclical patterns of popularity. Over a period of 750 years, says Allderidge, 'there are very few, if any, ideas on the public and institutional care of the mentally disordered which have not been round at least once before'. She cites the seventeenth-century as 'the first great era of Community Care', but realises that it could have been around much longer (Allderidge, 1979).

It is argued that the community approach, far from segregating those with mental health problems, allow them to be integrated within 'normal society' with their neighbours, and even where these ties have become strained or broken, would afford the re-establishment of social relationships (Scull, 1983): that is, to integrate them into the very society that once was seen as causing their mental health problems in the first place. And how has this complete reversal of philosophy been achieved? The answer lies in the historical development of the relationship between two groups of people – those who have mental health problems and the professional group of people who came to take charge of them, the psychiatrists.

It was the segregation of those who suffer mental distress which brought them under the wing of this rising professional group. It was within the institutions, isolated from the community, that a guaranteed market for the experts' services was established and thereby their 'craft skills' in the management of the mad could develop.

The asylum itself grew out of a need to establish a social order, which the rise of urbanised industrial society needed; the response was some form of institutional setting for which only the state could take the responsibility. So it was that the emergence of the asylum and a developmental link between medicine and insanity came to be seen as the natural outcome of this growing civilisation which elicited an increased humanitarian concern for one's fellow-men. It was after all non-productive to have the disruption of the lunatic within the workhouses.

> The mental hospital would be an asylum in a dual sense: to the workhouse it would afford relief from the disorder always at least latent in the presence of madmen; and for the maniac himself it would provide a sanctuary, a refuge from the world with which he could no longer cope (Scull, 1979).

The psychiatric profession meanwhile could lend scientific legitimacy to any critics of institutions, for their approach emphasised order and rationality, and above all self-control; that is, insanity could be captured and organised by shifting it neatly into the medical arena. This meant that:

Insanity was transformed from a vague, culturally defined phenomenon afflicting an unknown, but probably small, proportion of the
population into a condition which could only be authoritatively diagnosed, certified, and dealt with by a group of legally recognised
experts; and which was now seen as one of the major forms of deviance in English Society (Scull, 1979).

And so it was that the existence of both asylums and psychiatry
later came to justify the need and rightness of distinguishing the
insane from other deviants.

Yet it was far from proven that institutional care was better
than any other kind of care. This meant that only by emphasising
the expertise of the carers and the positive benefits that asylums
offered could advocates of these institutions make any case for
offering the 'benefits' to others who were not compelled to use the
asylums. Through the Mental Treatment Act 1930 voluntary patients who came to be attracted by this encroachment of the medical profession into the field of insanity, were to become and still
are the largest group of users of psychiatric care in Britain. It was
John Connolly who pointed out that it was not difficult to select
features of an individual's behaviour which could be interpreted
as evidence of his madness. By sending someone to an asylum
was to ensure that such an interpretation was correct: 'once confined, the very confinement is admitted as the strongest of all
proofs that a man must be mad' (Connolly, 1830). The creation of
more institutions, therefore, guaranteed the discovery of more
and more inmates to fill them. By 1990 the average asylum contained 961 patients, which had by 1930 increased to 1221 (Hume
and Pullen, 1986). Once the asylums had grown to colossal proportions, it began to be realised that those individuals who were
confined there came to lose their individuality, became part of the
order and guided by the institutional rules, so much so that their
ability to return to the society from which they came began to be
questioned.

> a gigantic asylum is a gigantic evil, and figuratively speaking, a manu-
> facturing of chronic insanity (Arlidge, 1859).

The building of state asylums had been urged by humanitarian
reformers who had laid claim to their therapeutic nature. Now the
reverse is true; the return of the mentally ill to the community is
also heralded as both humanitarian and therapeutic with the
same amount of enthusiasm as their removal had been. Accept-

ance of their return to the community has been made easy by concentrating on those earlier generations of patients who were admitted to Victorian asylums, thus making it easier to accept such drastic changes to the system. It also deflects attention away from 'the demise of state responsibility for the seriously mentally ill and the current crisis of abandonment' (Gruenber and Archer, 1979). Ideologically this is of profound significance because this development legitimised 'community treatment', not by careful demonstration of its merits (which would require systematic attention to its practical implementation); but by rendering the alternative simply unthinkable (Scull, 1983). And, as Allderidge shows, earlier attempts at community treatment failed. She writes:

> Community psychiatry did not actually work terribly well the first time around, as shown by the gradual move during the following century towards the next cycle of development – more hospitals (Allderidge, 1979).

Critics of this idea of cyclical patterns of care might want to argue that early seventeenth-century forms of community care do not bear any comparison to what is happening currently in Britain and America. Given that the care itself may differ in a wide variety of respects, there are nevertheless fundamental similarities related to administering care in a community setting that were valid then and are equally applicable to twentieth-century attempts. Two documents which draw the same conclusions appear in 1681 and 1975; the former being the Lancashire Record Office, Quarter Session Records, and the latter the Social Security's White Paper: *Better Services for the Mentally Ill* (DHSS, 1975). Both assure us of the recognition of significant social and environmental aspects of mental illness: especially highlighted are the problems with which relatives are forced to deal in order to keep a mentally ill relative at home. In other words these problems have remained untackled for over 300 years, which does not augur well for the current community-care attempts. No mention, however, is ever made of the bulk of mentally ill individuals who generally have no home, and few relatives.

Evidence from America should show how cyclical the care of the mentally ill is, for America now leads the way in patterns of care. The asylums emptied at a greater rate than in Britain and community care has had a longer experimental period (Bean and Mounser, 1989). Certainly, community care has not been a huge success and like the seventeenth-century experiment the cycle turns again towards the new era of hospitalisation – that is, not to build new asylums but to refill the existing ones which had never been completely closed.

The legal era

America had undergone a gradual move toward a legal era from the 1960s onwards. The 1960s and 1970s saw the rise in legal powers, where courts began to examine what went on in mental hospitals. In contrast to British and European civil commitment practices, the USA turned towards a legal model of decision-making which emphasised the 'due process'; based on the rights of the individual rather than on a medical model, as exemplified by British procedure. In this period if a person was found to be unfit to decide whether s/he needed medication or treatment, the recourse was to the courts where substantial judgement was applied. In many states it was judges and juries, rather than mental health professionals who actually made the decision to place or retain a mentally ill person in a psychiatric hospital for any significant period of time. Lawyers began to represent the patient aggressively and disturbed individuals were hospitalised against their will only if they were mentally ill and a danger to themselves or others. In addition, patients came to have legally enforceable rights: specifically the right to refuse drugs and other intrusive treatments such as electro-convulsive therapy (ECT) – psychosurgery almost disappeared.

In the post-decarceration days where 'community care' in all its fashionable forms had become well-established in America for much longer than it has in Britain and elsewhere, a discernible trend has begun to emerge which leads the way toward the twenty-first-century. The changes are away from this legal system which emphasised judicial oversight, and back towards a paternalistic medical model of 'therapeutic commitment'. Psychiatry has become more aggressive than in the 1960s and the 1970s. Psychiatrists themselves are no longer passive, they have grouped together; the Psychiatric Association has drawn up its own statute. At the same time families of people with mental health problems have also become active; by grouping themselves they can demand the treatment their relatives were unable to get under the old legal system. But it is being achieved by the increased use of coercion.

State legislature now enacts laws which permit coercive hospitalisation if it is considered necessary for treatment. Each state has its own laws, but basically the mechanisms are through police powers for assessment of dangerousness and *parens patrae*, where the mentally ill are admitted *before* they do anything harmful. Many courts, especially federal courts, are handing down decisions which indicate that mental-health professionals will have more power to provide the treatment they consider appropriate even if the patient objects. Since the early 1980s the law has given psychiatrists the role of social controllers; if they are seen to challenge this they actively devalue psychiatry. The great emphasis is to remove people from the streets, which in many American towns are becoming dangerous. Mayor Koch in New York has an active programme to collect all people wandering or sleeping rough on the streets and deposit them in a 1000-bedded night shelter – patients prefer to sleep rough because these places are more dangerous than the streets (Cohen, 1988).

This emerging trend is part of a larger social movement in the USA in which legislature and courts are currently engaged in legal reform aimed at strengthening the security of the community against violence committed by individuals. Reforms are being made in the criminal law (including changes in the insanity defence) aimed at minimising the opportunity of mentally ill offenders to avoid conviction and punishment. Consequently, the emphasis on individual liberty and legal rights and the accompanying judicial activism which seems prevalent in the 1960s and 1970s is fast receding. Whilst coercion forces people to take community treatment, e.g. out-patient treatment, there is also a 91 per cent increase in involuntary patients in Washington. Most of these have no previous psychiatric history (as measured by hospitalisation), which means that almost all had been managing on their own in the community somehow. This is what Durham and La Fond call the 'neo-conservative law and order era' where voluntary patients are unable to get hospital treatment in a time when the hospitals are once again full to overflowing (Durham and La Fond, 1988). In the USA the cycle turns once again.

Definition and doubts

It is clear that the term 'discharge' can no longer be defined in a neat well-ordered way as hitherto. That older version would involve a process whereby psychiatrists or the psychiatric team in the hospital would assess a patient's progress and decide whether he or she could be free to leave – the decision being made on clinical and social grounds; or whether the patient required post discharge contacts from the GP; or if not ready for discharge then whether the patient required new or additional treatments before being reconsidered and reassessed later. But matters do not happen like that anymore, at least not in England and Wales – or if they do then their hospital systems have not yet caught up with the pace of events. As we said before, everyone gets out, and some, it appears, whether they are ready or not; or indeed, whether they are able to live in the community or not.

Thus far we have avoided defining what we mean by a discharge and by being discharged. The way in which we use the terms here reflects policies in countries who have deinstitutionalised their mental patients: it involves more than being released from the mental hospital, it means ceasing contact with the psychiatrist or psychiatric team altogether. We define the terms this way because we believe the hospital, in a community-based system, ceases to exert the importance and influence it once had. Being relegated to a minor position, it is now one institutional setting among others. All are aimed at providing a support system for the main centrepiece which lies in the community. A community-based system is what now exists: in its advanced form, as in some parts of England and Wales, it is a system whereby patients make their first and last contacts with the treatment services. Patients may have nothing to do with the hospital services, or if they do they may enter the hospital for short periods before returning to continue their treatment in the community. Their treatment programme need not involve a spell in hospital, or if it does it need not do so to the exclusion of community-based programmes. Of course this was always the case as some patients were treated in the community. But under the new system of deinstitutionalisation, patients will not be treated and dealt with by hospital-based psychiatrists, or discharged from the hospital without further community contacts. Their hospital in-patient phase, where and if it exists, will be defined by community-based psychiatrists. Psychiatrists will maintain control of the patient when they leave the hospital. That is the essential difference. In our definition of discharge the patient leaving the hospital has not been discharged from care: the patient's discharge occurs later when the community psychiatric team decides to cease further patient contact.

It is misleading then to talk of patients being discharged from hospital as hitherto. We see the hospitals as letting out or transferring patients from one part of the system to another. Of course under the old system patients were discharged, though as we said earlier they may have first started their contacts in the community setting. A patient may have made his first contact with a GP, be sent to the mental hospital, admitted, treated, and then released back to the out-patient facilities. In one sense, of course, one could say that was no different from what happens today. Yet that would be to miss the point: the modern system only superficially operates in that way. Under the old system there were no community psychiatric teams to send the patient to the hospital, and the hospital adopted the central position in the treatment programme. Nor was there a community psychiatric team waiting to receive the patient on release – the same team incidentally which was responsible for sending the patient to the hospital in the first place and treating the patient during his/her stay there. The difference is not just one of emphasis. Under the old system the hospital was of central importance. Under the new it no longer directs, controls, nor dictates the pace of treatment or care.

Our definition of discharges and being discharged is therefore wider than before. Yet it still invites the same basic questions. How does a patient get out of the psychiatric system – as opposed to getting out of the hospital? How, and under what circumstances, are patients told that they are no longer required to attend this or that clinic or out-patient centre? Could it be that it might be more difficult to be discharged than before, for under the old system the line between in-patient and out-patients was more clearly drawn. Now it is blurred. Patients are likely to drift from one treatment agency to another or drift out of the system rather than experience sudden and dramatic release. They may even believe they remain within the system when they do not, or may believe they are discharged when they are not. To go from a hospital to an old people's home for example, need not involve any form of discharge as defined here but a transfer. That transfer tells us nothing about the patient's status or position *vis-à-vis* the treatment programme.

Presumably the patient in the old people's home is still part of the system? Might it be then that some patients are never discharged: once contact has been made with the system, might they remain in it for life? The new all-embracing, all-encompassing, all-pervasive treatment programme may have arrived at last when the patient remains on the programme and finds that he/she can never get off. Patients simply have their status as a patient reactivated at the switch of the community-treatment programme. Under the new system might it be that no one is ever fully discharged? Are we at the beginning of a new Orwellian possibility?

We do not know if things will turn out that way. And anyway we are not wanting to speculate too much; our aims are more modest. We wish to describe and analyse some of the changes that have already occurred and show some implications of those changes. We think that is as much as can be achieved at this stage given the paucity of the data and the abundance of opinion.

Let us be a little more specific:

- Consider proposals for a new Community Treatment Order (CTO), or rehabilitation programmes, or the Patients' Rights Movement perhaps. All have changed, or if not will be expected to change under the new system: the CTO in the USA has already extended hospital controls into the community with little apparent thought or consideration about what differences they might have, or whether they simply transfer controls from one setting to the other.
- How will rehabilitation programmes take account of the new Social Fund in Britain or similar provisions elsewhere which provide social security benefits, or access to the housing system. Rehabilitation no longer means training for release from the hospital in preparation for adjustment to community life, it means being rehabilitated whilst one lives and works in the setting in which the original problem was identified, i.e. the community.
- What are patients' rights in the community?
- Can and does the psychiatrist have different contractual obligations to patients living and working in their own homes, and what should be the corresponding duties of those administering the treatment? Community psychiatry and the discharge of patients in that community opens up new ways of thinking and new avenues of thought.

Sometimes it is difficult to see what these new positions and implications might be. It is easier and more understandable to contemplate the mistakes already made or to be gloomy about the path already taken. It is easier to regard the omens as unfavourable and the portents ill. As one commentator, Talbott, sardonically notes 'The chronic mentally ill patient has his focus of living and care transformed from a single lousy institution to multiple wretched ones' (Talbott, 1974). But, like ourselves, Talbott also notes that whilst every error imaginable has been made it is unthinkable to suggest a return to the old ways. We have proceeded too far to turn back now – and perhaps after all the failures were not so much due to ideological or philosophical deficiencies but to the manner of the implementation of the underlying ideas (Talbott, 1974).

We are not therefore concerned with discharges from hospital but being discharged from psychiatric care. Yet even that is too simple for at present we know too little about how that care system operates. It needs to be mapped and described and that is part of our aims. Having done so in Chapter 2, where we provide a general review of discharges, we move in Chapter 3 to consider community provision which is the link between hospital and community. In Chapter 4, sectorisation as the main method of working and treating patients is considered. Sectorisation is the new fashionable catch-all term, but we shall ask how it works and how patients get out of the system. Later we consider proposals for the new CTO looking closely at how it would operate and how patients would get off a Community Treatment Order. And later still we look at mental patients' rights and finally at the mentally abnormal offender asking how the patients can be discharged (in the traditional sense of the term), from prisons or Special Hospitals when there is no other place for them to go. In our concluding chapter we try to see what discharges mean for the future and how they are to be redefined. For clearly new definitions are needed whether of treatment programmes or whatever in the sense that the term is simply out of date.

One further point about definitions. Throughout we have tried to refer to comparative material and to make the book international in its perspective. But that is easier said than done. In a recent study of European Mental Health systems, for example, the World Health Organisation (WHO) found the definitions differed so widely that no one was sure what was what any more. For example what constituted 'Europe'? That was difficult enough – Morocco claimed to be part of Europe, as did Israel – but it was a minor problem compared with defining a psychiatrist (some countries meant psychologist, others a general practitioner who happens to treat people with mentally-disorders), a mental hospital could mean anything from a hospital with mentally disordered patients to a hostel with three patients. And what was mental disorder? Then there were the data: some European countries claimed not to have this or that type of problem when for political reasons it was too sensitive to admit the problem existed, others claimed to have a greater problem than was expected, presumably hoping for greater levels of international aid. And so it went on (Bean, 1988). One can imagine the additional confusion likely to arise discussing mental health legislation. What constitutes a compulsory order and a compulsory patient is anyone's guess.

We have tended therefore to stick with valid data, a lot of which is our own and collected as part of the research for this book. If that means relying on local studies so be it: we prefer this to other data which may be less valid although taken from a broader geographical area.

2
Getting Out of Mental Hospitals

As we said in Chapter 1, everyone now gets out of mental hospitals – though as will be shown later when we look at the Special Hospitals, this general statement needs slight modification. Even so the old idea of one group – probably the acute patient – being able to leave, and the other – probably the chronic patient – remaining on the back wards has passed. Acute and chronic alike find themselves out of the hospital together. Their fate unhappily is not always the same, nor always one about which we should be proud – although occasionally one forgets there was little to be proud about in the old hospital-based system either, especially for the long-stay chronic patients.

As will also be shown later, the decline in the mental-hospital population is statistically reflected in a greatly accelerated discharged pattern, using the term 'discharge' in a traditional sense. This is where the decarceration movement and community-care system meet, or rather should meet. According to Peter Sedgwick the community-care system may have influenced greatly the policy of admissions and discharges, but his view is that it does not in reality exist (Sedgwick, 1982). He seems not to be alone. The Second Report of the House of Commons Social Services Committee would agree: 'The pace of removal of hospital facilities has far outrun the provision of services in the community to replace them' (HMSO, 1985a). To many critics deinstitutionalisation or its corollary, community care, has been government policy in Britain, the USA and elsewhere for the past 30 years yet has in fact achieved very little other than a consensus about emptying the mental hospitals.

The deinstitutionalisation movement could not be justified simply on statistical or financial terms. It had to be reinforced by an ideology. Although we are not directly concerned with these matters, it is as well to note that there has been a growing conviction among many mental-health professionals that removal of people with mental health problems from 'normal home and community ties' reduces their chances of effective treatment. Moreover, institutionalisation has led to a belief that reinforced norms and behaviours promote a dependent role for the patient which makes it difficult to adapt within the community upon discharge. It was thought that if patient-care occurred in a familiar relatively stigma-free home environment, the patient would be more likely to be understood, and would be less likely to see himself as a stigmatised expatriate (Bachrach, 1976). Deinstitutionalisation is also the expression of a philosophy rooted in an era of social and political reform which strongly emphasised people's self-determination and the right to control the forces which affect their own lives.

Even among the advocates of the decarceration movement fears exist that patients leaving hospital are being dumped in the community leaving them isolated and physically and socially worse off than before (Scull, 1977 and 1983). Whether this is so or not the movement itself has had a natural history of its own; that is, it was a logical response to what might simply be called 'the times' (Bachrach, 1976). 'The times' were an era of great social–political conservatism, yet paradoxically of great social and political reform. 'The times' which occurred in the late 1950s and early 1960s emphasised changing the individual and modifying the environment. This was the impetus behind community care.

Sadly we have learned that keeping patients at home may not mean just keeping them out of hospital – despite the fact that in earlier times hospitalisation may have been seen as necessary for their treatment. Phasing out hospitals has also meant phasing out patients without providing an effective alternative. Some critics have argued that people with mental health problems have gone from the frying-pan into the fire. Under the guise of one ideology patients in public mental hospitals have been transported to another setting i.e. the community. Few would dispute the view that mental hospitals had long since become dehumanised through neglect, and had failed to meet patients' needs, but turning patients back into the community itself does not make the second wrong right. 'In today's world neglect in the community dwarfs neglect in hospitals.' (Slovenko and Luby, 1974). By 1991 the Department of Health closed 60 of Britain's psychiatric hospitals, thereby reducing the 70 000 hospital beds to 43 000 (Cohen, 1988). When we say 'everyone goes out of hospital' we mean that with only 43 000 available beds left turnover must be rapid.

Discharges at the national level

Using the British figures, which, despite many defects are probably at least as valid as those of other countries, we can see that Britain has gone a long way towards deinstitutionalisation. The first and most obvious point to be made is that in Britain, or more specifically England and Wales, the mental-hospital population has shown a consistent and dramatic decline. From a high point in 1955 of 165 000 patients dropping to 120 000 in 1965 it will be expected to reach 43 000 in the early 1990s (HMSO Mental Health Enquiry, 1986).

The debate about the future of mental hospitals goes back at least to 1961 when Enoch Powell (the then Minister of Health) said the intention was to reduce the 150 000 mental hospital beds (42 per cent of all hospital beds) by half by 1975 and to locate those that remained in general hospitals. He believed that the new developments in psychotropic drugs would help to speed up this decline. He seemed not to have noticed that the decline in in-patient numbers had begun much earlier, before the introduction of these drugs. Nor did he, or others who supported deinstitutional-isation, acknowledge the fact that such a decline could not continue unabated. There would always be some patients who needed to stay in hospital. It is, as Andrew Scull says, as if much of the time policy-makers simply do not know what will happen when their schemes are put into effect. Nor do they seem very concerned to find out (Scull, 1977).

Certainly Sir Keith Joseph shared Powell's view, when he announced the new policy; he believed the drug evolution to have changed the treatment of most psychiatric conditions (see Bean and Mounser, 1989). Drug treatment was, he thought, able to effect real cures. Enoch Powell had earlier advocated the reduction of psychiatric beds from 3.4 to 1.8 per thousand population: his successors were more enthusiastic: even by 1971 beds were reduced to 2.0 per thousand population.

If measured simply in terms of reducing the number of beds in mental hospitals, then implementation of the Government's policy has been effective. The Mental Health Enquiry of 1986 revealed that in the twenty years between 1955 and 1975 some 56 000 beds in psychiatric hospitals were closed. In the next ten years (up to 1985) a further 24 000 were closed, and another 17 000 were expected to go by 1991 when, it was estimated, there would be 43 000 beds left for psychiatric patients – 100 000 less than in 1955. Table 2.1 sets out the data.

Table 2.1   *Mental hospital beds in England and Wales, 1955–91*

	1955–91
Year	Hospital population
1955	143 000
1965	120 000
1970	111 000
1975	87 000
1986	60 000
1991	43 000 (Projection)

Source: HMSO, Mental Health Enquiry, 1986.

Table 2.2   *Admissions to mental hospitals in England and Wales, 1965–85*

Year	Admissions
1965	156 213
1970	272 931
1975	175 111
1980	180 200
1985	199 995

Source: HMSO, Mental Health Enquiry, 1986.

Paradoxically, in spite of this reduction the hospital admission rate rose in England and Wales. There were, for example, 155 000 admissions in 1964 compared with 179 000 in 1976. Table 2.2 shows the admissions for this period. It will be seen that the number of admissions – i.e. patients admitted for the first time – have been increasing especially since 1975. (Patients admitted for a second or subsequent period will be treated as 'readmissions'.)

How can this be? The answer lies in the patients' length of stay. Whereas in the 1950s the average length of stay would have been about 6 months – and 12 months or more was not unusual – by the 1980s it had dropped to between 1 and 2 months. It was particularly this characteristic which allowed large numbers of beds to be closed (DHSS, 1975).

However, the reduction of beds would have been greater had not there been a second factor, a rise in the readmission rate. Table 2.3 sets out the readmissions to mental hospitals since 1972.

Table 2.3 *Readmissions to mental hospitals in England, 1972–86*

Year	Readmissions
1972	115 034
1978	120 456
1979	120 073
1980	127 184
1982	132 893
1985	146 900
1986	145 900

Source: HMSO, Mental Health Enquiry, 1986.

The general conclusion from these figures is that the number of mental patients has been reduced overall, as has their length of stay. At the same time the hospital admissions rate has risen, particularly for those patients who were readmitted on numerous occasions. This is shown for example by the 80 per cent of the 24 705 discharges patients who left hospitals in London in 1981 who had been admitted at least once before (GLC Health Panel, 1984).

Of course, this demonstrates the national pattern of in-patient flows; local variations exist which also have to be considered especially since statistics at the national level are subject to a variety of elements which can make them far from valid. Data available from Nottingham will be given in a later chapter and will provide a means of showing the differences between local and national data. For example, our data from the Nottingham Psychiatric Case Register shows a decline in aggregate numbers of admissions between 1980 and 1985 of 18.8 per cent compared with 1.4 per cent nationally. One possible explanation is that the data is Nottingham have been collected systematically and are more comprehensive than these available nationally. At this stage we wish to set the scene nationally and show general trends.

When we look more closely at the national data it is clear that trends are more complex than at first apparent. It is too simplistic to say 'everyone gets out' of mental hospitals because this ignores a number of features related to the process. Some patients leaving mental hospitals will have been admitted during the period dominated by the decarceration movement. Others leaving mental hospitals have been long-stay residents and were admitted prior to the current philosophy. Obviously the processes involved in their departure will be different. For the former – the recent admissions – it is likely to mean a return to the community under community psychiatry with which they are familiar (see 'Sectorisation' in Chapter 4). For the latter – the long-stay patients – it is likely to mean a move to another form of care (and control) in an old people's home (Part III accommodation), private nursing homes or hostels. Or if they are sent directly into the community they are not only sent to a new psychiatric regime of care, but are returned to a community which is alien, at least, to them. Table 2.4 shows the number of patients leaving hospital in relation to their length of stay in hospitals.

Yet when we talk about discharges we often forget about those patients who die in mental hospitals, for they are likely to be chronic in both a mental and a physical sense, and will probably have been in hospital a very long time. Table 2.5 shows the corresponding number of patients who died while in hospital in relation to the number of years spent in hospital.

Table 2.4   *Number of patients leaving mental hospitals and units and length of stay (deaths not included), 1972–86*

Duration	1972	1979	1980	1982	1983*	1985*	1986
All	165 455	158 684	168 907	172 720	178 300	188 700	188 400
< 1 month	86 786	92 791	100 840	104 363	109 800	116 900	115 900
1 month –	54 680	46 529	48 367	48 386	48 600	50 300	50 200
3 months –	16 938	14 543	14 760	15 088	15 100	16 300	16 800
1 year –	4 644	3 443	3 488	3 630	3 500	3 500	3 700
5 years –	1 341	793	766	697	700	800	900
15 years +	1 066	585	686	556	600	800	900

* figures are approximate.
Source: HMSO, Mental Health Enquiry, 1986.

Table 2.5   *Deaths in mental hospitals and units and length of stay, 1972–86*

Duration	1972	1979	1980	1981	1982	1985*	1986*
< 1 month	2 873	2 298	2 458	2 320	2 400	2 500	2 400
1 month –	1 868	1 661	1 694	1 722	1 800	1 800	1 700
3 months –	2 476	2 304	2 346	2 437	2 400	2 400	2 300
1 year –	3 949	3 370	3 391	3 468	3 400	3 400	3 200
5 years –	1 731	1 437	1 289	1 321	3 400	3 400	3 200
15 years +	1 914	1 408	1 478	1 230	1 200	1 300	1 200
Total	14 811	12 478	12 656	12 498	12 300	12 400	11 800

* figures are approximate.
Source: HMSO, Mental Health Enquiry, 1986.

The death rate in mental hospitals has fallen by 12 per cent over the last decade and follows the pattern for admissions. However, of the 11 800 people who died in hospitals in 1986 more than 90 per cent were over the age of 65 years.

The nature and number of patients leaving hospital under decarceration

At a national level the number of patients leaving hospital under decarceration depends on the extent to which each country has advanced the policy of closure of mental hospitals. This in turn is usually dependent on the corresponding development of 'community care' – though it may not always be. As already explained, in a district like Nottingham, decarceration has meant a decline in the number of beds, which has in turn produced a decline of 18.8 per cent in admissions, compared with the national figure of 1.4 per cent. Some districts are slow to advance this policy, or perhaps they are much wiser to slow the pace of change.

Under the decarceration movement most patients spend only a short time in hospital. In Britain in 1986 115 900 patients left hospital after less than one month – representing 62 per cent of all patients leaving hospital that year. Hence as we have already said, decarceration means that everybody or nearly everybody gets out of mental hospitals: the main issue now is what happens to them after leaving. The British figures show that over the past decade the pattern has changed most for those patients who are 75 years and over – we expect the same situation to exist elsewhere as one of the inevitable consequences of decarceration. Short stays in hospital for this age-group have increased by 250 per cent since 1976, much more so than for the 65–74 age group. However, explanations of this phenomenon cannot merely be attributed to central government policies or changes in service provision, other factors influence this trend. First, the number of people over 75 years old has increased in the general population in Britain by 30 per cent since 1976. Second, the use of short-periods in hospital for this group in order to give 'carer respite' has been not only a consequence of a community care policy but also perhaps contributor to promoting it, for 'carer respite' has always been a feature of the mental hospital function.

The decline of 28 per cent in people resident in British mental hospitals since 1976 has been influenced by the number of deaths in hospital each year, as well as the number of long-stay residents who have left. The current policy of not admitting chronic patients for lengthy periods means that this long-stay institutionalised population now being discharged will be finite in number; it means also that the kind of accommodation it will require, and the level of state-sponsored support will be of short duration. These new chronic patients who would, under the old system have become 'long stay', will have different needs again. They will have lived in the community (in one sense of the word or another) and therefore not become 'institutionalised' in the same way as the long-stay inmates of old. The kind of accommodation they have, and will need in the future, together with the level of support/care may be significantly different. These differences in needs should be monitored, we believe, in order that the right kind of care, support and accommodation is available for the future.

That is not to say that other groups of patients' needs should not be monitored also. We think it just as important, especially as the decline in hospital beds and the speed at which they are disappearing mean that people needing hospitalisation will soon be unable to get it. This has been an inevitable consequence of decarceration, where it has occurred. The increased readmission rate with a decreasing number of hospital beds available cannot go on forever. The time will come or has already come when the talk will be, or is, of bed shortages, and we believe that day is nearer in places where 'Community Care' policies have been running the longest.

Rehabilitation, aftercare and statutory provision

A great deal has been written about the manner in which patients leave mental hospitals, the failure of care in the community and the lack of overall policy towards mental health whether in Britain or elsewhere. The House of Commons Select Committee Report of Community Care (HCSCCC) provided a damning indictment of the failure of central government to provide adequate funding for the mental health services, and clear policy guidelines for the implementation of the closure of large hospitals and the transfer of services to the community:

> Any fool can close a long-stay hospital: it takes more time and trouble to do it properly and compassionately. The Minister must ensure that mental illness or mental handicap provision is not reduced without demonstrably adequate alternative funding being provided beforehand both for those discharged from hospital and for those who would otherwise seek admission (HMSO, 1984–5).

But what should go in to preparing patients for life in the community? Presumably some sort of rehabilitation programme. But what is that? We have something of a hint of it in the Griffiths Report 1988 where the point was made that Community Care was aimed at ensuring an optimum quality of life for individuals leaving hospital (HMSO, 1988). The Report provided an official statement of the problems that are faced by patients, professionals and statutory bodies involved when patients leave hospital. It is especially relevant to mental hospitals where patients are more likely to be additionally stigmatised by the nature of their illnesses as well as by their potential financial or social status. The assurances for the future contained in the report lie in ensuring that:

- the right services are provided in good time, to people who need them the most;
- the people receiving help will have a greater say in what is done to help them, and a wider choice;
- people are helped to stay in their own homes as long as possible, or in as near a domestic environment as possible, so that residential nursing home and hospital care is reserved for those who needs cannot be met in any other way. (HMSO, 1988)

The high ideals of such a document fall short because little attention is given to the small details, provisos and exemptions that the relevant statutory provisions maintain. Too often the various systems, such as the benefits system, or the housing system, or the employment system, or the education system, work in isolation, follow their own codes and regulations, are in practice inflexible and work mutually to exclude each other (see Chapter 3). The health-care system – which in the case of patients who leave hospital and need to settle in the community is probably the most flexible – has to approach the other systems in order to accomplish the task that Central Government has set it: that is, to send its patients into the community and close the hospitals – a task that at most times is difficult, but with the new State approach to welfare benefits and housing has become almost impossible (Mounser and Bean, 1990; Bates and Walsh, 1989).

Deinstitutionalisation refers to a wide range of patient-based events which range from carefully planned local efforts to achieve this expressed ideal, to the more easily recognised mass release of patients into the community, which is largely unprepared for them, from the state hospitals which in Britain are now being phased out. In some cases, as we have already said, those patients released have received little or no preparation prior to leaving hospital; in other cases they have undergone programmes – e.g. rehabilitation – which do exist but are able to accommodate only a handful of patients compared with the total number of patients sent into the community (see Lavender and Hollway, 1988, ch. 14).

It is clear that there is a need for a variety of approaches for aftercare in order to meet the variety of responses in the population to be served. It is no longer just a question of how we can humanise the system; rather, what is the best procedure for which kinds of patient. Once there is a variety, informal choice becomes possible for the patient. Barnett argued against falling into the trap of prescribing a new monolithic system for the present, no matter how 'humanised' the new system may appear to be. A monolithic system (i.e. one without variety and choices) cannot be a humanised system (Barnett, 1975).

Rehabilitation has become entrenched in our society and has already achieved an established position in the care of the mentally ill. Rehabilitation is not undertaken in isolation from other people; the realities of the outside world are considered and treatment is extended to the community prior to resettlement.

> The aim of rehabilitation is to restore the individual to his maximum level of independence, psychologically, socially, physically and economically (Hume and Pullen, 1986).

Rehabilitation is the process by which a person is helped to adjust to the limitations of his disability and where lost skills can be regained through the development of coping strategies.

It implies, therefore, that something has been lost, that can be regained, and that this can be accomplished by some form of 'training'. What had been lost was seen very much as caused by entry and long stay in institutions, for people began to realise that patients who spent many years in hospitals were likely to become institutionalised by its regime. If hospitals were to close as decreed, then some measure to alleviate the debilitating effects of institutions needed to be sought.

In fact, not only did the development of what came to be known as 'institutional syndrome' severely hamper the goal of deinstitutionalisation, but multiple admissions also generated 'stigma' which acted against the successful transition of the patient from hospital to the community. This institutional syndrome described by Barton (1959) and Goffman (1961) consisted of apathy, lack of initiative, loss of interest in events not immediately personal or present, submissiveness, lack of expression of feelings or a resentment of harsh or unfair orders from the staff, a loss of individuality and a deterioration in personal habits, toilet and general standards. Passivity and apathy arise as a result of the disease process itself, by a restricted life style prior to admission and the effects of institutional life itself. Admission separates the patient from the outside world and takes over all decision-making for the patient whilst the hospital functions for its own self-preservation.

Barton highlighted several aetiological factors which he associated with this institutional syndrome. Loss of contact with the outside world, with personal friends, possessions and personal events like birthdays, was the main debilitating factors. More importantly, entering an institution for any length of time severely endangered one's prospects outside the institution. Other factors related to the staff – for example, the ward atmosphere – he also considered highly debilitating (Barton, 1959). The implication of such arguments led advocates to the conclusion that the removal or reduction of such debilitating factors could only occur outside the institution where the patient would be less likely to lose personal friends, possessions and personal events – that is, he would be in contact with the real world. Rehabilitation evolved to assist the transition of those patients already in institutions and to facilitate their disposal to the community.

However, the words that are used in a rehabilitative context often become confused; for example, words like 'diagnosis', 'need' and 'therapy'. There is often a failure to recognise the differences between these and others like 'treatment' and 'training', and also 'reform' and 'rehabilitation'. In fact, rehabilitation and reform have become interchangeable. Francis Allen warned of 'the delusive simplicity and ambiguity of the notion of reform' (Allen, 1959), whilst Roger Hood made a useful distinction between 'training' and 'treatment':

> Training means a conscious effort to influence attitudes of others, whilst 'treatment' seems to imply a method of dealing with the problems of the individual (Hood, 1966).

The first is related to external controls whilst the latter means the internalisation of values acquired through significant contact with someone else, e.g. a therapist:

> essential in the public's interest is that the mind of the individual be studied and its difference in function from the normal mind of the socially conforming should be understood (HMSO, 1967).

The first question that comes to mind here is, of course, what is the 'normal mind of the socially conforming'? And further, what are the implications of coercion in social conformity?

The American Correctional Association believed that the proponents of rehabilitation did not rule out the necessity of custodial segregation, but considered custody as a means to an end in the vast majority of cases, and an end in itself in a very few cases. They do not, however, deny the desirability of achieving a deterrent effect if it can be achieved without impairing the effectiveness of the rehabilitative programmes (American Correctional Association, 1972). Yet reform is claimed to be a humanitarian philosophy, although Richard Cloward argues that we cannot say that humanistic exercises are automatically reformative (Cloward, 1960); often humanitarian considerations and rehabilitation may conflict (Bean, 1976).

Those who have mental health problems are seen as deviant, and therapy, to Berger and Luckmann entails the application of conceptual machinery to ensure that actual or potential deviants stay within the institutional definition of reality (Berger and Luckmann, 1967). But what is reality, and whose reality are we talking about? A report for MIND emphasised the importance of tracing patients who have left hospital, and evaluating their experiences. This would allow ex-patients' views and wishes to be taken into account in service provision (Reid and Wiseman, 1986). Likewise, Scull argues that reliable information about the whereabouts of patients is of vital importance, yet policy-makers have not yet recognised this in the 'confusion and ignorance that surrounds deinstitutionalisation' (Scull, 1985).

In keeping with this view Goldie examined the experiences of decarcerated mental patients which showed clearly that the patients and the staff with whom they were used to mixing when they were in institutional care, inhabit quite different social worlds (Goldie, 1989). Furthermore, there is much evidence to suggest that where some staff work and almost live with their patients for years they still know very little about their patients. Such a lack of knowledge is compounded by the fact that the staff themselves become products of the institutions in which they work and are often not in a position to judge the abilities of their patients to live outside. Of course, the same staff are now emerging also from these institutions and taking up roles as community carers in the new scheme of things. They too may find it difficult to accustom themselves to functioning in a therapeutic milieu in which they have had little experience.

There are coercive elements of rehabilitation even for the mentally ill who may be institutionalised against their will and as has been argued elsewhere:

> Under the influence of the rehabilitative ideal, questions about justice have been ignored, and in some quarters seen as irrelevant (Bean, 1976).

Particularly vulnerable are the group of long-stay, long-term users of psychiatric services. This group of people are almost by definition seen as 'failures' of existing services. They have had multiple or long-term admissions, with long periods of residence in psychiatric institutions, with an accumulation of various disabilities and disadvantages which make them especially susceptible once the mental hospital ceases to exist (Goldie, 1988).

Rehabilitation requires professionals to make judgements at certain key points in the rehabilitative process which means that they usually posit a consensus model of society. The 'rehabilitative ideal' has generated more demands for social workers and psychiatrists, together with a range of other professionals, to treat more of the people with mental health problems and to encroach on the penal system. This expansion of professionals who deal with the groups of long-term users of the psychiatric services has produced what Goldie recognised as an 'amalgam of different occupationally based expertise'. Yet there is, he argues, a lack of consensus in the policies that ought to be persuaded to deal with them. It is the diversity of this 'expertise' which produces conflicting views about what should be done. Not only are there major differences between the staff involved with the clients of these services, but there is an even bigger gulf between the staff themselves (Goldie, 1977).

Yet the rehabilitative ideal is not one basic model, there are numerous models which exist and rehabilitationists might disagree amongst themselves about the emphasis to be placed on each of these models. For example:

Some psychiatrists would use the organic model in their treatment of mental illness, whilst others would operate within the principles of diagnostic/treatment models and claim they are treating a behavioural disease which they conceive an analogous to an organic disease (Bean, 1976).

Models of mental illness

Among the models of mental illness that exist the following are perhaps the most common, and therefore the most used in psychiatry today.

1. The *organic model* explains that psychiatric conditions are the result of some underlying physical condition. For example, serious infections such as pneumonia can produce acute confusional states, whilst abnormalities of the thyroid and pituitary can cause mood disturbances. Yet few psychiatrists would argue that all mental illness can be explained in this way, and considerable debate has grown over the issue of whether schizophrenia is an organically based illness. This argument has been forged by the relatives of schizophrenics who do not wish to be stigmatised by Laingian theories which claim that schizophrenia is caused by the family.

2. The *psychotherapeutic model* emphasises the importance of early childhood experience which may have a bearing on the emergence of psychiatric conditions in later life. Unsuccessful completion of developmental stages in childhood, it is argued, leads to a re-emergence of emotional and relationship difficulties experienced early in life. This includes fixation at stages and regression from other stages. This may help to understand neuroses but there is little evidence in existence to show that psychotherapeutic measures are effective. At the same time it fuels the arguments about the inadequacies of parental socialisation and seems to fix the blame for later problems back with the family.

3. The *behavioural approach* describes behaviour as being 'learned' and states that behaviour which produces the most pleasure is seen to be reinforced, whilst that which produces less pleasure is extinguished. There is the implicit denial of the 'unconscious' in this model. It is often seen as helpful in the treatment of phobias and obsessions, where certain behaviour directed towards certain objects or experiences is 'unlearned' by the use of rewards and punishments.

4. The *social model of mental illness* looks at the individual in relation to his social situation. Concepts such as 'labelling' and primary and secondary deviance are used. Deviant behaviour (primary deviance) may lead to someone being labelled 'mentally ill'; once the label is accepted – i.e. by admittance to hospital – abnormal behaviour may follow (secondary deviance). This model has encouraged the emergence of the therapeutic community movement, and aims to understand people in terms of the environment in which they live.

5. The *medical model* takes account of the symptoms, syndrome or disease, as well as the person who suffers, his personal and social situation, and his biological, psychological and social status. Like other illnesses it is seen as the environment working on the organism and is not to be confused with the social model (Clare, 1980). Yet, as Kathleen Jones discovered in her study of discharged psychiatric patients, the programmes/plans for these people tended to be limited to a single service and tailored to short-term needs. Often discharge plans were not recorded and seldom lasted for very long after discharge (Jones, 1985).

Rehabilitation is based on the medical model, but adopts other treatment approaches where they are applicable. Thus, a man being resettled after developing schizophrenia may receive medication (medical model) in a hostel run on therapeutic community lines (social model) whilst receiving social skills training (behavioural model) (Hume and Pullen, 1986).

Data on the nature and extent of rehabilitation programmes are difficult to obtain. The extent of such programmes which exist within our own area of experience in Nottingham, particularly, have a large network of influence within the statutory, voluntary and private resources within the district, as well as expanding provision within the health services of both residential and day-care facilities. However, it is much harder to describe the effectiveness of such rehabilitation programmes in terms of outcome, and whether they have affected or improved the quality of the discharged patients' lives. Residential rehabilitation programmes are expensive; estimated by Bates and Walsh to be on average in excess of £20 000 for an average length of rehabilitation (Bates and Walsh, 1989). Those chosen for such pre-discharge programmes will inevitably be selected as being likely to benefit from it; and numbers will be correspondingly small.

In Nottingham in 1985 a total of 1825 patients were sent out from mental hospitals or units. Of these only 50 were given in-patient rehabilitative programmes with a further 20 returning to ordinary acute in-patient care for unknown reasons. Similarly in 1986 there were 1744 patients from hospital/units with only 44 of these having specialised rehabilitative care. Eighteen additional patients returned to acute in-patient care that year. Whilst these numbers do not in any way reflect a failure of rehabilitative programmes in Nottingham, they perhaps highlight the lack of significance that is traditionally afforded to preparing patients for departure. The rehabilitation team in Nottingham have a wide network of influence in the community and once discharged (in the traditional sense) from in-patient care, the community team does not remove any patient from their books, but monitors their progress in the community indefinitely. Patients, therefore, are never discharged (in the sense we use in this book), and so the number of patients in contact with rehabilitation in this district is continually growing.

Other reasons why residential rehabilitation is so small is em-phasised in Chapter 3 which shows that difficulties of actually getting patients placed in the community are exacerbated by the benefit system and the housing situations (see Bates and Walsh, 1989).

The transfer of monies from the closure of hospital beds and the sale of the old asylums is failing to find its way to the area most needed, i.e. preparing for and maintaining patients in the community. The only significant transfer of funds has been in staff resources; the staff have moved out into the community to work in a new way.

Planning for leaving the hospital

The exodus from the mental hospitals described above rarely involved individual planning – indeed stories abound of patients leaving as if they were being evicted from the mental hospitals! One US hospital released nearly 3000 patients in about 3 months. There was no sense in which one could talk of planning for departure in those circumstances.

But to what extent were, and are, patients involved in, or part of, any planning for departure? In more sedate times one could imagine the situation to be roughly like this: the patients' progress through hospital would have been monitored and their progress noted. An assessment would have been made of each patient's mental and physical state, with similar assessments made of the social situation to which the patient would return – whether for home and family, employment, key social relationships or anything else regarded as important. At a critical, but prepared point, the patient would have been discharged – perhaps for a trial period, perhaps not – later to take his/her place in the outside world. That, at least, was what was supposed to happen. Strangely enough we know of no research on the so-called discharge process which would show whether this occurred or not. But we doubt anyway that many patients ever left in such an ordered and organised way. Anecdotal evidence suggests that the number of planned discharges were small. A few patients may have had their discharges planned in the manner defined here, but we think that these were rare. Other patients, perhaps equally few, were sent out because they were a nuisance to the hospital. A similar number absconded, and another similar number left against medical advice (perhaps no one was prepared to do anything to stop them). Finally some patients were sent to other institutions (the elderly to Old People's Homes or what we in Britain call 'Part III Accommodation', whilst disruptive patients were sent to Special Hospitals in secure accommodation, etc.). Most of the remaining patients we think, left, because they were ready to go and the medical and allied nursing staff agreed. In the institutional-based system, little was planned in the formal sense, there was simply an agreement that the patients were ready to leave.

It is perhaps a recognition of this lack of planning that at last governments have begun to show some interest in patients leaving hospitals. (In Britain this has been prompted by reports about patients who have left and have subsequently committed serious offences.) The ideal-type programme fostered by the British Government taken from a Department of Health Document has a blueprint which is as follows:

- It is important to recognise that modern psychiatric practice calls for effective interprofessional collaboration.
- It is important that proper arrangements are made from determining what services are assessed as necessary care, and whether appropriate resources can be provided.
- The explicit agreement of all those, including carers, expected to contribute to a patient's care programme is essential.
- It is important that proper opportunities are provided for patients themselves to take part in discussions about their proposed care programmes, so that they have the chance to

discuss different treatment possibilities and agree the programme to be implemented.
- Where a care programme depends on the contribution of carers,
it should *always* [italic original] be agreed in advance with the
carer who should be properly advised both about such aspects
of the patient's condition as is necessary for the support to
be given, and how to secure professional advice and support
both in emergencies and on a day-to-day basis (Department of
Health, 1990).

It is no accident that the Department of Health document
attempts to define, for the first time, the procedures – that is, itself
making us further suspect that nothing along these lines ever
happens or has ever happened in practice. There have, of course,
always been regulations and laws governing the manner in which
patients leave the hospital subject to compulsory powers under
the Mental Health Act 1983, and some will be dealt with in later
chapters. Those not under compulsion have been entitled to leave
at any time, (except where Section 5 of the Act is enforced which
gives the hospital the right to hold the patient for three days if the
hospital does not consider the patient is ready to leave). The
Department of Health document is doing more than just setting
out procedures. It is trying to establish a link between the hospital
and the community so that once an assessment has been made of
the patient he can be treated outside the hospital. The Department
of Health Document suggests that the most effective means
of undertaking a post-release programme is through a case-
management system, with named individuals, often called 'key
workers' identified to carry the responsibility in respect of individual patients.

A similarly 'ideal type' of procedure has been identified in the
Mental Health Act Commission Code of Practice (HMSO, 1990)
which we include because it is one of the few government documents to deal with the question. This is under the heading of
Aftercare – the purpose of which is defined as enabling a patient
to return to his home or accommodation other than a hospital or
nursing home, and to minimise the chances of his needing any
future in-patient care (HMSO, 1990, para. 26.1). Section 117 of the
Mental Health Act 1983 requires health authorities and local
authorities, in conjunction with voluntary agencies, to provide
aftercare for certain categories of detained patients. The Code of

Practice goes on to talk of planning for aftercare, presumably again concentrating on detained patients, but perhaps not exclusively so. It says this:

> When a decision has been taken to discharge or grant leave to a patient, it is the responsibility of the RMO to ensure that a discussion takes place to establish a care-plan to organise the management of the patient's continuing health and social care needs. This discussion will usually take place in multiprofessional clinical meetings held in psychiatric hospitals and units. If this is not possible, administrative support should be available to the RMO to assist in making arrangements (HMSO, 1990, para. 26.6).

Who should be involved in the discharge process? The Code of Practice provides a list similar to that of the Department of Health, namely:

- the patient's RMO;
- a nurse involved in caring for the patient in hospital;
- a social worker specialising in mental health work;
- the GP;
- community psychiatric nurse (CPN);
- a representative of relevant voluntary organisations (where appropriate and available);
- the patient if s/he wishes and/or a relative or other nominated representative.

And what should their considerations be? The Code of Practice puts it:

> The multiprofessional discussion should establish an agreed outline of the patients' needs and assets taking into account their social and cultural background, and agree a time-scale for the implementation of the various aspects of the plan. The plan should be recorded in writing (HMSO, 1990, para. 26.10).

Those contributing to the discussion should consider the following issues:

- the patient's own wishes and needs;
- the views of any relevant relative, friend or supporter of the patient;

- the need for agreement with an appropriate representative at the receiving health authority if it is to be different from that of the discharging authority;
- the possible involvement of other agencies e.g. probation, voluntary organisations;
- the establishment of a care plan, based on proper assessment and clearly identified needs, in which the following issues must be considered and planned for insofar as resources permit:
    day-care arrangements;
    appropriate accommodation;
    out-patient treatment;
    counselling;
    personal support;
    assistance in welfare rights;
    assistance in managing finances and if necessary claiming benefits.
- the appointment of a key worker from either of the statutory agencies to monitor the care-plans implementation, liaise and coordinate where necessary and report to the senior officer in his/her agency any problems that arise which cannot be resolved through normal discussion;
- identification of any unmet need (HMSO, 1990, para. 26.9).

The Code of Practice aims to provide a general set of guidelines about which practitioners can consult and base their decisions. We should not therefore be too hard on it or criticise too severely the blandness of its stated objectives, and its occasional ambiguities and inconsistencies (e.g. patients' 'wishes and needs' are required to be considered as if they were one and the same). Moreover, the idea that there should be recorded plans for all patients leaving hospital is a little optimistic. Even if the plans were confined to the smaller number of compulsory patients there would be many thousands annually. Indeed we do not know of any positive sightings yet of such planning and we eagerly await some. That apart, the Code of Practice as the major document from the Department of Health has set the stall out and moved the debate along a little further.

Events have also moved things on; one was a particularly tragic case which led to a social worker being killed by hospital in-patient, and a subsequent Committee of Enquiry (HMSO, July 1988 – the Spokes Report). Again the details here are important for they illustrate the problems involved in the decarceration movement and the tensions this produces as well as strains in the community. Briefly, on 6 July 1984, Miss Isabel Schwarz, a social worker employed by Bexley Council near London, was killed at the offices where she worked at Bexley Hospital, Kent. She was killed by a former client, Miss Sharon Campbell. Sharon Campbell had been an in-patient at Bexley Hospital, a psychiatric hospital, between June and September 1980 and again between August and November 1982. From September 1982 until October 1983 Sharon Campbell had been a social-work client of Isabel Schwarz. The death occurred some 9 months *after* Isabel Schwarz ceased to be Sharon Campbell's social worker. On 8 July 1984 Sharon Campbell was arrested for the murder of Isabel Schwarz, and on 22 August 1985 a Court Order was made under Section 51 of the Mental Health Act 1983 committing Sharon Campbell to Broadmoor Hospital on the finding that she was not mentally fit to stand trial. On 9 March 1987 the Secretary of State for Social Services appointed an Inquiry (under Section 84 of the Mental Health Services Act 1977 and Section 250 of the Local Government Act 1972) with terms of reference which were 'to inquire into the management of arrangements for the care and aftercare of Miss Sharon Campbell, to consider the adequacy of these arrangements and to report' (ibid, p. 1).

This Inquiry (the Spokes Inquiry) was largely concerned with the unique and tragic circumstances that led to the death of one social worker. Nonetheless it saw itself as moving from what is called 'this unusual case' to consider general problems of discharged patients – especially those likely to be violent. The Inquiry noted a significant number of changes in the intervening years between Isabel Schwarz's death in July 1984 and its Report in July 1988, namely, an increasing recognition of the need to provide longer-term hostels as well as short-stay hostels, and increasing awareness of the need to provide accommodation and employment or a place in a day-centre. Most of all, and following on from the Code of Practice (2nd Draft August 1987) there was, said the Spokes Report, a need to continue multidisciplinary reviews of patients which involve planning for discharge and follow up (HMSO, July 1988).

The Spokes Inquiry made a number of recommendations which are of general importance. The first concerns social workers who have statutory duties to supervise patients who have left hospital. It recommended that the Secretary of State issue to health and local authorities a written summary clarifying their statutory duties and provide aftercare for former mentally disordered hospital patients. The second requires the Local Authority to make arrangements to provide social-work support and other domiciliary and aftercare services to persons living in their own homes, or elsewhere, who are or have been suffering from mental disorder. Thirdly there should be a social work devised plan at the time the patient is discharged which should be clear and recorded in the social work notes. It should be communicated to others who need or may need to know its contents (para. 8.22). Fourthly social-worker supervision should be planned supervision on the basis that the choice of cases for discussion should be that of the supervisor while of course giving to the social worker being supervised the opportunity to discuss cases where he or she wants help or advice – this to avoid the situation where difficult and unsuccessful cases are kept away from the supervisor (para. 8.23).

Similarly the Inquiry recommended that before the patients left hospital an in-patient treatment plan should be prepared by the psychiatric team. The plan, especially for those whose effective and efficient aftercare presents problems (i.e. patients admitted for brief periods under treatment orders, or under assessment or emergency orders, or others who are vulnerable but not under formal orders) should also require the Social Services Department to cooperate in providing adequate aftercare. It would be part of the plan to establish a register of such patients in the appropriate catchment area and the responsibility of the consultant psychiatrist to keep that register up to date.

The emphasis of the Spokes Inquiry was on planning: whether it be planning for discharge by a single agency (Social Services) or planning through a multi-agency or through a multi-disciplinary team. A further recommendation of the Spokes Inquiry was that the Royal College of Psychiatrists be invited to publish a document on good practice and aftercare for ex-hospital patients. Such a document was to be published after seeking a consensus with bodies representing nursing, social work, general practitioners, psychology and occupational therapy (para. 16.19).

In October 1989 the Royal College issued its guidelines – the first of its kind on this particular topic. Interesting though these guidelines are, and in spite of their historical significance, they tend to reproduce the same message as the Spokes Inquiry. That is, good practice must be based on a careful multidisciplinary assessment of the patient after which a plan for aftercare should be prepared which is fully understood both by the patient and by those concerned with their care. After the patient has left the hospital the aftercare plan must be regularly reviewed and updated. Decisions made after such a review must be recorded and communicated appropriately. Some vulnerable patients, whether admitted on orders or informally, require particular care in the planning of their aftercare for which a systematic record should be used (Royal College of Psychiatrists, October 1989). For the homeless, or itinerants, special attention must be given to review those patients who may be lost to follow-up and everything possible done to find out what has happened to such a patient and the appropriate action taken (Royal College of Psychiatrists, October 1989).

There is nothing wrong with these recommendations as such, and if implemented they will be worthy additions to matters of patient care. But they illustrate a more general point which needs consideration for it affects all matters relating to the way patients are sent out of hospitals. Our major criticism is not what is said but rather what is not said. The guidelines seem to be a bureaucratic device to solve the problem. There is nothing more. There is, for example, no attempt to consider recent developments of treatment in the community – except in the most general sense, – or to consider changes in hospital admission rates, readmissions, or rates of 'discharge'. There is nothing about sector treatments, the mentally abnormal offender, nor of homelessness, nor even of the Community Treatment Orders. There is nothing about rehabilitation, and no attempt to distinguish between leaving hospitals and being provided with aftercare. There is, however, a great deal about record-keeping, and interdepartmental conferences (all to be run and supervised by consultant psychiatrists of course!) and a nodding recognition of the problem of confidentiality, but even that is quickly passed over. (How much information on the patient's psychiatric condition should be given to other members of the interdisciplinary team? What should that information consist of and why should it be given? Would it be of a different nature than, say, for those patients leaving a general hospital?) These and other questions could have been tackled – and in our view should have been tackled if the matter is to be dealt with properly. The changing nature of patient-care will not be met by interdepartmental conferences and meetings with members of multidisciplinary teams.

3
Community Provision and the Link with the Mental Hospital

In this chapter we wish to open out the discussion about what happens when patients are dealt with in the community. We are concerned here with the direct link between community provisions and discharges (in the sense used here) from hospitals. As shown in Chapter 2, the process of leaving hospital should involve preparation for life in the community. That it does not is one of the failures of the present system, but that will be dealt with by other volumes in the series.

Treatment in the community

It is often taken as axiomatic that any kind of life in the community is better than remaining in mental hospital; but on leaving hospital patients go to various types of situations, not all of them good. Patients with mild psychiatric conditions, good family support and favourable financial situations may be expected to be generally better-off out of hospital. Yet those with serious or florid symptoms, little or no family support or who have financial problems are likely to be worse off. The *New York Times* editorial on 8 April 1975 summed up the plight of those patients first turned out of mental hospitals in the USA:

> But what kind of crusade is it to condemn sick and fearful people to shift for themselves in an often hostile world; to drag out, all too commonly, a hungry and derelict existence in a broken-down hotel if they are lucky; victimised, if they are not, by greedy operators of so-called halfway houses that are sad travesties on a fine concept? All without their even knowing the possibilities of new medical approaches to their illness – and all in the name of civil liberties (*New York Times*, 1975).

It is often forgotten that at their best mental hospitals provided nutritious but institutional food, good personal care for those who cannot care for themselves, and excellent professional health care. They supported and protected their patients, providing the function of 'sanctuary' in an otherwise hostile (for them) world. Hospitals kept patients occupied and provided group leisure activities, making sure that they were not isolated, and provided them with physical environments ranging from the bare and shabby to the luxurious, depending on whether upgrading had been carried out or not. Much of this the ex-psychiatric patient will complain is lacking, even in the pseudo-institutional substitutes of the private and public homes. Currently, mental hospitals do not provide a stable environment, since a policy of rapid discharge means that patients have no control over whether they stay there or not (Jones, 1985).

The quality of life lived by the patient and his relatives is, after all, the final criterion by which services must be judged. A good hospital is better than a poor hostel or a poor family environment; or a good family environment is better than a poor hospital or hostel. Both these philosophies have ruled and survived at one time or another, only to be abandoned with little or no true evaluation. The same may be said of day-time environments like open employment, enclaves in ordinary commercial business, rehabilitation or sheltered workshops, or protected day-centres. Universal denunciation of any one type of setting is likely to be harmful since it is clearly not based on rational principles of assessment, treatment or care (Wing, 1975).

In America, as Cohen points out, many of the homeless were ex-patients who could not manage in the outside world. Now there is a new population of people who have never been in hospital, but who need treatment. He says that both streets and shelters are full of individuals who show symptoms of acute mental illness, some are withdrawn, some are very exhibitionistic. But he argues that the diagnosis does not matter very much as the care for these people does not exist (Cohen, 1988). Some would argue that it is not a question anyway of needing psychiatric care, but a housing problem; for these people are rootless, homeless and alienated from normal society. Whereas in the past this new population of people with mental health problems would eventually find themselves in hospital, if the hospitals are all to close, where will they now find the treatment they may need? If the system is to operate through general practice then treatment is dependent upon whether each person has a general practitioner or not, and whether their illness can be contained within a stable community environment. If they have no sense of community, however, this approach will not work.

In Britain studies have shown that between one-quarter and one-third of all illnesses treated by general practitioners are diagnosable as mental disorders (Clare and Shepherd, 1978), and that about 15 per cent of the adult population at risk present to their general practitioner with a mental disorder in any one year (Shepherd *et al.*, 1966). This has engendered arguments that there is a need for psychiatrists to collaborate more effectively with GPs to promote community mental-health care. This is particularly so with the growth and development of community mental-health centres which can be used as an illustration of the need to collaborate if services are to be appropriate.

Community Mental Health Centres (CMHC) are an export from America. They are locally-based centres for the delivery of psychiatric and related services to people with mental health problems, who are now no longer treated in mental hospitals. They provide a base outside the hospital for the multidisciplinary team and the provision of a wider range of services than those of the more traditional structured day-care facilities. Depending on the emphasis of the Centre – and there are various kinds in existence – they may offer walk in, crisis, prevention or consultation services (Boardman, 1988).

Locally-based centres in the United Kingdom are typically referred to as:

1. Community Mental Health Centre (CMHC)
2. Mental Health Resource Centre (MHRC)
3. Community Mental Health Resource Centre (CMHRC)
4. Mental Health Advice Centre (MHAC)

By 1987 there were 122 centres either existing or planned with assured funding, and 155 at the unfunded planning stage (Sayce, 1987). Their objectives vary according to the emphasis of each centre, but CMHC are more likely to involve psychiatrists than are MHRC which are likely to be Social-Service-led. However, NUPRD argue that the distinction may not necessarily be found in practice (Sayce, 1987). The centres surveyed by NUPRD fell into three distinct categories, notably:

1. those which were *the devolved psychiatric service*, being the entry point for most of the locality's mental-health referrals

and offering a full range of assessment, therapeutic and treatment services;
2. those operating *a low-key sessional model*, offering counselling and/or group-work, sometimes on a part-week basis and sometimes in conjunction with a day-care service;
3. those operating *the community development model*, with an emphasis on initiating networks of care with other agencies and generating self-help activity, rather than on direct service provision.

They found that the second type of centre, the low-key sessional model, formed a slightly larger group than the other two. It seemed that the more comprehensive type (the devolved psychiatric service model) was the most likely to target people with long-term mental health problems and the community development model (number three) to pursue strategies for user and community participation.

In the USA, however, where the CMHC movement has had 15 years more experience than in Britain, there has been a distinct fragmentation and loss of perspective, which has led to a significant exodus by the psychiatric profession and ultimately to sharp cuts in funding of such centres under the Omnibus Reconciliation Act 1981 (Okin, 1984). This has happened in a milieu where there is less confusion of terminology and less variation in the type of centre, which were mandated to provide five specific services (unlike Britain where the Department of Health and Social Security has not as yet produced a definition of the term or any specific guidelines).

The failure of the CMHC movement was largely attributable to the entrenched institutional practices which prevented more thorough planning. CMHC and state hospitals failed to coordinate the two major mental-health delivery systems, mainly because of both institutional competition and uncoordination, and because of professional disputes over the direction of psychiatric care.

However, two of the American developments emerging in Britain are first, the tendency for CMHC to neglect people with long-term, serious mental health problems in favour of preventive and acute work, and second, their relative lack of commitment to the consumer movement, as indicated by involvement of users or community representatives in central decision-making (Sayce, 1987). One of the adverse consequences of the expansion of mental-health concepts in the 1960s which is still relevant in the

1990s was this redirection of attention from the needs of the psychotic patient. Community mental-health centres had diffuse missions and found it easier, or perhaps professionally more re-warding, than dealing with the more difficult patients, to focus on assistance for those with less severe disorders (Mechanic, 1975).

Britain's CMHC seem to be providing counselling, psycho-therapy and health education rather than those services which are traditionally seen as relevant to the long-term group i.e. rehabil-itation, occupational therapy or employment schemes. As research conducted in Lewisham has shown, what is happening with the opening of accessible centres with a broadly defined target group is that more people are being seen by mental-health services overall, an increase which is accounted for mainly by people with emotional or situational disturbances who were previously seen only by general practitioners (Boardman *et al.*, 1987).

> The USA centres' tendency to concentrate on counselling the 'worried well', arguably a more rewarding task for professionals, may thus be being repeated in England (Sayce, 1987).

At the same time community-based services may not be relev-ant to some ethnic groups, and this may result in underutilisation. Rural patients, elderly patients and those of low socio-economic status may be difficult to deal with and cater for. Myers and Bean found that 'adjustment in the community is more difficult for lower-class patients' (Myers and Bean, 1968). Community treat-ment needs to be geared to the cultural needs of the patients it serves or, more importantly, are in need of it.

A survey by the MHAC showed neuroses (28 per cent) and transient situational disturbances (24 per cent) to be the diagnoses most frequently encountered and a further 22 per cent of patients diagnosed as having personality disorders. The more serious psy-chiatric disorders like schizophrenia (4 per cent) and affective psychoses (6 per cent) were being seen less often. These findings remained during the two years reviewed, but transient situational disturbances rose considerably in the second year along with personality disorders (Brough and Watson, 1977)

The most common aim of the centres was 'accessibility', which was encouraged by the use of ordinary houses and the use of a drop in service or at least a theoretical acceptance of self-referral. Yet some critics have argued that a highly visible and significant new problem evolved because of concentrating service facilities in certain areas of neighbourhoods, to the point of possible community saturation (Wolpert, 1975), whilst others have shown that community services may be less accessible than the hospital-based services in a variety of ways (Bachrach, 1976). Community services may operate limited business hours at CMHC or primary-care premises, or greater time, distance and financial resources may be needed for patients to travel to them. Yet, accessibility, together with an emphasis on prevention, constitutes CMHC's most significant departure from traditional hospital-based services. The Lewisham research not only shows clear success in increasing accessibility, but also shows that Mental Health Advice Centre (MHAC) users received more effective and efficient treatment than a control group referred to local out-patient departments (Boardman *et al.*, 1986). However, one-quarter of all the centres seemingly had no links with the local community which given that they call themselves Community Mental Health Centres, shows that this title has little meaning related to their activity.

There is, however, no doubt that Mental Health Advice Centres have been dealing with individuals in a highly distressed condition, mostly people in acute stages of neurotic illness or transient situational disturbances. It is here that the general practitioners assume greater importance. Most of these referrals come from general practitioners, but there is an increase in self-referrals. Moreover, the large number of non-emergency referrals to the centres from local general practitioners suggest that these centres and their mode of working is affecting changes in the model of referrals suggested by Goldberg and Huxley. Their model of psychiatric referrals using a one-year period prevalence suggested that 250 people out of every 1000 have some form of psychiatric problem, but of these only 230 will present to their general practitioner and only 140 are likely to be recognised by him/her as mentally ill. Of the 140 recognised by the general practitioner to be mentally ill only seventeen would be referred to a psychiatrist, six of whom would be admitted to a mental-hospital or facility (Goldberg and Huxley, 1980).

Goldberg and Huxley suggest that the second and third filters – i.e. the GPs' ability to detect psychiatric disorders among patients and refer them to psychiatric services – may simply be consequences of the present service organisation. A change in this organisation could effectively modify their model of referrals. Evidence from MHAC already suggests that this kind of innovation in community psychiatry is serving some individuals not previously dealt with by this specialist service and, Goldberg and Huxley would argue, therefore meeting previously unmet needs.

> Increasing demand for community psychiatric facilities in recent years has suggested that radical changes in the organisation and delivery of mental health services may be necessary if these demands are to be met, even partially (Brough *et al.*, 1988).

It has been shown that the majority of psychiatric assessments take place in out-patient clinics at district general hospitals at the request of general practitioners. However, the clinic referrals are a small proportion of the patients with psychiatric complaints or associated problems, since 95 per cent are managed without specialist help (Shepherd, 1974).

The effectiveness of the psychiatric help provided by the primary-care service has been questioned for some time (Brook and Cooper, 1975) and it has been suggested that psychiatrists should collaborate more closely with general practitioners and their primary-care services (World Health Organisation, 1973). The practical ways of achieving this would be for psychiatrists to hold regular sessions in health centres (Corser and Ryce, 1977; Brook, 1978) and attachments by psychologists (Johnstone, 1978) or social workers (Cooper *et al.*, 1975; Corney and Briscoe, 1977; Shepherd *et al.*, 1979) to general practitioners to form an expanded primary-care team. However, few general practitioners make direct psychiatric referrals to other professionals e.g. social workers, psychologists or community psychiatric nurses, and even fewer have the opportunity for case discussion with a consultant psychiatrist at their own surgeries (Furlong *et al.*, 1988).

It is arguments like these that we would want to look at very carefully, and to ask certain questions. For example, how is it that under this model general practitioners are represented as being so unable to diagnose psychiatric illness – after all, they are the ones with the most consultations for such illness? There is also much evidence to suggest that a large proportion of the psychiatric problems seen by general practitioners are intimately related to adverse life events and difficulties (Tenant *et al.*, 1981), hence the large numbers of transient situational disturbances and neurotic patients attending MHAC. From such findings we would want to ask if these patients were really suffering from mental disorders?

Furthermore, one of the requirements of medical training in Britain is at least six-months' experience with a psychiatric speciality, which one would expect would give doctors some guidance in recognising mental disorder. It has been mentioned elsewhere, that even the police who deal with a high proportion of acutely mentally disturbed people have considerable experience as 'diagnosticians of the mentally disordered' (Bean, 1986). Under Section 136 of the Mental Health Act 1983, a police constable can detain a person 'who appears to him to be suffering from mental disorder and to be in immediate need of care and control'. They have, therefore, a legal right to make a diagnostic decision (Bean *et al.*, 1991).

It has been shown that the police are, in fact, quite accurate in making this type of diagnostic ascertation (Bean, 1980); all but one of the patients held by the police were compulsorily admitted to a mental hospital. The remaining patient, although known to the psychiatric services, had a note appended to his hospital casenotes to the effect that because of his disruptive behaviour he was never to be admitted to hospital even if, as at the time of this study, he was clearly mentally disturbed!

Whilst the police have no formal training in such matters as diagnosis, even the Butler Committee recognised the efficiency of the police as referral agents (HMSO, 1975). The report quotes a study by Gibbons which concludes that the police are rarely wrong in using Section 136, indeed, they were more often than not aware of the patient's psychiatric history (HMSO, 1975, paras 9.10–9.12). A further study by Sims and Symmonds (1975) which looked at psychiatric referrals from the police, although not under section 136, found that the police tended to refer a high percentage of psychotic patients, of whom 40 per cent were ultimately found to be diagnosed as schizophrenic.

A more recent study of Section 136 by Rogers and Faulkner (1987) and Bean *et al.* (1991) found that 90.5 per cent of the referrals were considered by the psychiatrists to be mentally ill, indicating that the police were accurately identifying the presence of mental disorder according to conventional psychiatric standards (Rogers and Faulkner, 1987; and Bean *et al.*, 1991). These and other studies confirm police ability to diagnose psychiatric patients as efficiently as other professionals (see also Berry and Orwin, 1966; Mountney, Fryers and Freeman, 1969).

It is interesting, to speculate upon why the police should be so reasonably efficient as diagnosticians of mental disorder. Their expertise could stem from their considerable experience in dealing with people who show bizarre and odd behaviour. Yet general practitioners are called upon to deal with the same kind of behaviour when patients are admitted under Section, often having to make the decision to call in the expertise of the psychiatrist.

Clearly arguments about general practitioners failing to recognise mental disorder are founded upon a different group of the mentally disordered, the more acute and severe leaving no room for doubt. Often, as Goldberg and Huxley point out, at the initial stage of consultation with a general practitioner, it is impossible for the doctor to make a definite diagnosis. In Britain, the Royal College of General Practitioners' Research Committee (1958) estimated that firm diagnosis could only be made for just over half of patients seen (Goldberg and Huxley, 1980). However, it is unusual for general practitioners to refuse to recognise the patient as being ill even if they cannot diagnose the illness and will often accept the patient to be temporarily ill and treat his symptoms accordingly.

Community provision for discharged patients

In Britain the Audit Commission study team reported that the build-up of community-based services has been slow and is not keeping pace with the rundown and closure of long-stay institutions in the NHS. As many studies have indicated the lack of aftercare facilities is a feature of most services for people with mental health problems, yet the importance of effective post-crisis care cannot be stressed too highly as a preventive measure against hospital readmission (McLean, 1988). Like so many studies Catherine McLean found that half the people interviewed had no idea of the services that were available to them anyway.

Patients who are leaving after long-stay residence in large mental hospitals, have significant problems initiating and maintaining contact with the array of service-providers. It has been argued that lack of communication between the providers of such services frequently results in absent, duplicated or inappropriate services and those patients who are in most need of such services become lost once they are returned to the community (Faulkner et al., 1984). Yet, where Social Services have been utilised it would seem that they are the ones used most until the patient has been rehoused into the community, which is primarily at times of crisis. Moreover, it is apparent that additional support is necessary if these individuals are to live at adequate standards in the community (Wells, 1985).

Delman states that services for people suffering chronic mental-health problems 'should be the vehicle for a process, without time limitation, that fosters relationships of mutual help and support and instils a strong sense of responsibility' (Delman, 1980). Others would argue that rehabilitation is more than a process which seeks to reduce disability and develop compensatory abilities in individual patients. It also recognises that adaptation of disabled people depends on changes in the social environment. Support is necessary to sustain this adaptation especially when threatening life experiences might be expected to break down this adaptation (Bennett, 1983). The implications for the development of services specifically designed for populations of people with chronic mental-health problems are obvious, yet it is not merely a question of talking these people through a crisis. The integration of all the services available within each statutory agency is of paramount importance.

We will now look at some of these services available in Britain to illustrate some wider points about the importance of a set of sources designed to meet problems, other than those seen in psychiatric terms. These services are wider than those usually considered appropriate to ex-hospital patients yet it is these types of sources which we think are of equal if not more importance than the others. Indeed failure to consider these has been one of the blights for most of the debates about patients leaving the mental hospitals.

The benefits system

In a more practical way the Social Fund, introduced on 11 April 1988, was expected to give support to the aims of 'community care' that the Griffiths Report highlighted. It replaced the system of single payments of supplementary benefit used to help people with exceptional expenses that could not be met from normal income (Becker *et al.*, 1988). The Social Fund introduced instead the Community Care Grant which was intended to promote this idea of 'community care' by helping individuals to live independent lives. It provided for one-off payments to help people who were leaving institutional care, or to help others to remain in the community and not to enter institutional care if it could be helped. Such grants are at the discretion of Social Fund Officers, and are paid from a fixed monthly budget. The priority groups it aims to reach are elderly people; people suffering mental handicaps or other mental-health problems; those who are physically disabled, chronically sick or terminally ill; alcohol and drug addicts; ex-offenders requiring resettlement; people without a settled way of life (i.e. the homeless), families under stress and young people leaving Local Authority Care. Of the numerous grants available the 'start-up grant' is particularly important to patients leaving mental hospitals, for it is allocated to allow the recipients to provide themselves with the necessary furniture, bedding and household equipment to live in an independent dwelling. To qualify for such a grant the person has to be receiving Income Support; this means that anyone receiving another benefit, like Invalidity Benefit, will not qualify at the outset. Unfortunately this will include a great many patients in mental hospitals and therefore, the Social Fund becomes beneficial to only a small group of people who actually need it (Mounser and Bean, 1990).

Claims made by the operators of the Social Fund include a 28-day time-limit for processing applications. This is important for psychiatric patients because this 28-day time limit has to tie in with the discharge procedure which may not always, even with the potential for flexibility which the hospital might have, be possible to synchronise. This point was taken up by the Griffiths Report when it said that prior to the introduction of the Social Fund there was 'insufficient clarity of responsibility for the arranging of publicly provided services in line with people's needs and service priority' (HMSO, 1988). Indeed, it emphasised the need 'to improve planning and communication between different bodies, so that the appropriate range of services is readily available to patients when they are discharged from hospital' (HMSO, 1988).

As yet, as the Report by Bates and Walsh shows, these particular problems have not been resolved. It is a point upon which the whole concept of 'community care', especially its success, rests. If the procedure for discharge and rehousing of patients is haphazard, then they will be unable to settle in the community; if there is no proper organisation prior to discharge then 'Community Care' will not work (Kay and Legg, 1986), and patients will find themselves returning to hospital, a point which can be demonstrated by current readmission rates to mental hospitals. As shown elsewhere the problems that disrupt the discharge procedure of patients from mental hospitals can seriously exacerbate the problems currently being experienced in both Britain and America with the rise in homelessness (Mounser and Bean, 1990). The health care professionals can only achieve so much given the restraints placed upon them by other statutory agencies, but it seems a strange phenomenon in the current climate of 'caring' that the situation can arise whereby patients are discharged onto the streets (Mounser and Bean, 1990), for Kay and Legg are right when they say that no patient should leave hospital without suitable housing having been arranged, that this should be after a thorough discussion of the various options available, and advice regarding welfare benefits and medication is of crucial importance (Kay and Legg, 1986).

> Life is hard for the newly discharged member of the community. Often there is no cooker in the flat, there may be only a mattress on the floor and little by way of carpet or curtains. Some people find themselves living on their own without even a television or radio after many months of communal living with ready access to both. Most people are too embarrassed to invite others into their accommodation, and so become even more socially isolated. With no prospect of improving their environment (weekly subsistence benefits do not provide enough to permit saving) there is little wonder that some people return to hospital (Bates and Walsh, 1989).

The Social Fund automatically excludes people who receive the top two rates of Invalidity Benefit, which means that those patients leaving hospital have no access to cash for furniture and general equipment needed to take up a tenancy. This situation, say Bates and Walsh, is not peculiar to Nottingham: in Birmingham the proportion of rehabilitation patients receiving Invalidity Benefit was 70 per cent in 1987, whilst the figure for Surrey and Northumberland was 85 per cent. In Nottingham 60 per cent of rehabilitation clients were found to be excluded from the Social Fund (Bates and Walsh, 1989).

This situation may force hospital managers to reassess their selection procedures for such services as rehabilitation, for if patients are to receive this expensive service, calculated by Bates and Walsh to cast an average of £20 000 for each period of residential rehabilitation, then it would be feasible to admit patients who are already receiving the type of benefit which would entitle them to the necessary help at the discharge stage.

The housing system

Many people leaving mental hospitals will need to find somewhere to live and are potentially homeless. Those who have been in hospital for many years may never have had a home of their own or may have lost it through being in hospital so long. This does not mean to say that patients who spend short periods of time in hospitals do not suffer loss of housing, for the very nature of admissions to hospitals can be very disruptive and some may lose their accommodation before they are discharged.

The study of Kay and Legg of homeless psychiatric patients in London, showed that by far the greatest problem for these people was their housing situation. As mentioned elsewhere (Mounser and Bean, 1990) 80 per cent of this sample were dissatisfied with their accommodation and 75 per cent wanted their own independent housing in the future. Of this sample 64 per cent had found their housing situations to have changed when they came to be discharged from hospital and the majority of these had eventually been discharged to institutional or 'supported' accommodation. The majority of these who had had independent accommodation when they were admitted had lost it whilst in hospital, their landlords having relet it in their absence (Kay and Legg, 1986). As Kay and Legg say:

> For the majority of those interviewed the period in hospital had dramatically altered their housing situation. An important issue is the role of their discharge in either resolving or creating housing problems (Kay and Legg, 1986).

People with mental health problems often also have a variety of social problems with which they are ill-equipped to cope, yet they are competing for housing with other homeless or potentially homeless people, in the same housing market. The problem for all homeless people is exacerbated by whatever housing policy is established at any given time. The policy of closing down mental hospitals coincided with a policy in the housing arena of providing accommodation for families; the emphasis on housing for single people has diminished. Many of the patients being discharged from mental hospitals (and, in direct parallel, from prisons also) are single, which means that they are likely to suffer additional discrimination in the housing sector. Between 1966 and 1971 the number of single households grew by 30 per cent, which included a 20 per cent growth in flat-sharing because of a number of single people under the age of 30 years in the general populations as a whole (Burke, 1981).

The policy of removing cheaper accommodation which attracted single people, especially those likely to be living on benefits, and the encouragement of building or renovating family dwellings, has had dramatic effects at this lower end of the housing market. The Housing (Homeless Persons) Act 1977 (consolidated in the Housing Act 1985 Part III) whilst it represented statutory recognition of 'homelessness', shifted the emphasis of the problem from that of a 'social' problem, to one of 'housing', yet no additional means to address the problem seemed to be forthcoming. Certainly no concomitant expansion in the housing stock was made to accommodate the huge numbers of patients being discharged from mental hospitals. Moreover, little recognition was given to the need to house what would, after all, be a long-stay population. So the building of hostels, for example, which one would have expected to cater for the initial numbers of people, did not happen. Local authorities who had the mandate to develop more hostels resisted this initiative on the grounds that this transitory (as they saw it) way of life should not be encouraged lest people grew accustomed to such a rough and self-destructive way of life. In the period between 1965 and 1972 the number of beds in hostels and lodging houses fell by 17 per cent at the same time as the decrease in numbers of psychiatric hospital beds.

The question that remains is: where have all those ex-mental-hospital patients gone?

Clearly, accommodation is of special importance to such ex-hospital patients and it is here that they often meet problems. A high percentage of people suffering from a long-term mental illness are single and they are competing for housing with a high proportion of the general population who are also single. Different areas in Britain have different problems in allocation of housing. A study of mental health, housing and community care in Tower Hamlets exposed the more acute problems of the mentally ill because of the high proportions of both single people and the mentally ill living in the area. Housing in Tower Hamlets consisted of 82 per cent Borough-owned dwellings with only 4.6 per cent owner-occupation in the 1980s. In 1984 57 per cent of the people on the waiting-list for accommodation wanted a one-bedroomed flat or bedsit. By 1986 the waiting list for accommodation reached the 10 000 mark while almost 1000 families were recognised as homeless and placed in temporary accommodation (Tower Hamlets, 1986). The Psychiatric Rehabilitation Association in 1966 showed the admission rates for all patients to hospital in Tower Hamlets to be 38 per cent above the national average.

Although mental illness could have some effort on an applicant's position on the waiting-list if the District Medical Officer judged that there were medical grounds for higher priority, in practice it rarely has any significant effect. The Tower Hamlets Report highlighted the importance of an effective housing service for vulnerable people, including those with mental-health problems, which would need to show renewed commitment and imagination. Their recommendation was for certain properties to be designated as being for vulnerable tenants who ought to be grouped together to enable adequate support to be provided. In order to facilitate such a project it would be essential to have closer cooperation between the housing departments, housing associations, health and social services and the voluntary sector.

Liaison between the hospital and the community-based facilities

With the exodus of patients from mental hospitals and the move by mental hospital personnel to units attached to general hospitals, the mental-health-care systems which have evolved have become complex. To the patient this may mean a confusing array of care facilities which are fragmented and not so easy to cope with. The more widespread the services become the easier it is for patients to become lost – one part of the service believing another part to be looking after the patient. At the same time mental hospitals have a more clearly defined social structure making it easier to understand statuses and roles within it, and establishing norms of behaviour within the hospital. When care is transferred to the community, traditional definitions no longer seem to work and 'anomie' (a social condition characterised by a general breakdown, or absence of norms governing group and individual behaviour) results (Hoult, 1969). It has been stated that the person with chronic mental-health problems does establish and generally maintains a stabilising role in the hospital which he has not been able to accomplish in the community even on a minimal level (Saunders, 1974).

It has, for a long time, been argued that the vast majority of patients currently cared for in state hospitals could be adequately treated in the community if a comprehensive spectrum of psychiatric services and residential alternatives were established (Becker and Schulberg, 1976). Yet the social functions of state mental hospitals are not necessarily the same as those publicly declared purposes and goals of these functions. The principal functions expected of state mental hospitals have included:

1. public safety and the removal from society of individuals exhibiting certain kinds of socially disruptive behaviour;
2. the provision of custodial care for persons who by reason of mental disorder, cannot care for themselves or be cared for elsewhere.

Treatment and rehabilitation of the mentally ill has traditionally been at best a secondary function of the state mental hospital, and for many years was not considered part of the function of the hospital at all.

Treatment and rehabilitation are considered the primary function of the mental hospital by those who work within them (Edwalds, 1964). The medical model terminology has been misleading, because when we use the term 'hospital' we automatically think of measurement. In fact, hospitalisation without treatment seems a conflict of ideas. Yet if we think of 'hospitalisation' as nothing more nor less than asylum ('sanctuary' seen as a place of refuge or safety) as the mental hospital was once called, there is no connotation of medical treatment, but rather one of treatment in the broad sense as meaning 'handling of' or 'how we treat one another' (Slovenko and Luby, 1974).

It is unclear what functions are to be transferred from the mental hospital to the community. Deinstitutionalisation has failed to provide functional alternatives for these basic functions of the mental hospital. In America this lack of alternative provision for the custodial elements of the hospital has led to a reversal of decarceration. Custody and asylum, if these were the needs of people with mental health problems, will not just disappear with the dismantling of custodial facilities. This has been proved in the USA where currently the large mental institutions are being filled by formally admitted patients in order to solve the very real problem of social control on the streets in America.

The emphasis of community care has always been on providing treatment in the community and not on custodial care of asylum. Community programmes often preselect patients to fit in with criteria set by experimental design. At the same time some of the custodial functions that the hospital provided has been taken up by private and public homes, at least for those over 65 years of age. In functionalist terms the question becomes one of identifying the appropriate functions of mental hospitals and the provision of alternatives in the community on a widespread, not just local, basis.

At the same time there is a need to target groups for deinstitutionalisation and to identify which patients are to be provided with community care:

- Do we mean *all* patients in mental hospitals or do we mean specific ones with certain demographic or diagnostic characteristics who can be assigned to certain community programmes?
- What about those patients who were hospitalised because there was no where else to put them?
- Have adequate alternative facilities been made available?
- Are we to concentrate on those patients who are a 'good risk' for rehabilitation via the community route?

Reform movements often create more problems than they solve. The task of each succeeding generation is to correct the excesses of the last. There comes a time when reformist zeal must be matched against available data, and if those data do not exist, they must be planned for at each stage of reform in order to evaluate such change. Whilst humanistic goals may persist, the ways to achieve them must be modified. At no time in history has consistent evaluation been applied to assess any system for the care, custody or treatment of people with mental-health problems. Momentous decisions have been made about people's lives, which have reversed hitherto accepted ways of treating people into inhuman and barbaric treatment, and all in the name of civil liberty and humanitarianism. Yet alternatives have not always been more humane. Reform has always seemed to be about changing the system or supplanting it with another. 'Reformers' have not concentrated on correcting the 'errors, faults or imperfections' of institutions or systems, but have instead tried to remove or abandon them, more often than not in favour of something much worse.

The special problem of elderly people

Elderly people were the first to be considered for deinstitutionalisation. The positive impetus was achieved by reversing the former practice of using state hospitals as 'a last respite before death' (Brown, 1985). In the USA the initiative began much sooner than in Britain. A 56 per cent decrease in the in-patient population between 1969 and 1974 was largely due to what Brown calls the 'transinsitutionalisation' of the elderly who were discharged from mental hospitals into mini-institutions within the community. In some States the decrease was much more marked; Alabama and Illinois reduced their elderly populations by 76 per cent between 1969 and 1974, California by 86 per cent and Massachusetts by 87 per cent. In Wisconsin, the discharge of 98 per cent of the patients aged 65 and over left a mere 96 of the original 4616 patients still in hospital (US Senate, 1976). During this period there was a 48 per cent increase in the number of nursing-home residents with mental disabilities – from 607 400 in 1969 to 899 500 in 1974 (National Centre of Health Statistics, 1975).

In USA, therefore, nursing homes, boarding homes and single-room occupancies (SROs) have become the principal residences of mentally ill persons. Over the past fifteen years, they have supplanted state hospitals in this respect. Efforts of reformers in the 1950s to abolish the traditional 'out of sight, out of mind' function of state hospitals have merely succeeded in creating mini-institutions in the community which replicate many of the custodial and dehumanising elements of asylum life (Brown, 1985). In Britain a study of long-stay patients in York (over one year in hospital) and elderly confused patients discharged to the community found that only five out of thirty-four were living 'in the community' in the sense that they had an ordinary domestic life in their own homes. The rest were found to be in some form of care in smaller and less formal units than a mental hospital ward, but lacking both the medical and nursing facilities and the activity programmes which a hospital could provide (Jones, 1985).

Wolpert, Dear and Crawford wrote about the fate of deinstitutionalised patients in a section of San Jose, California, where approximately 10 per cent of the population was composed of 'discharged patients who are indolent and living in board and care facilities' (Wolpert, Dear and Crawford, 1974). Moreover, the needs of the chronically ill patients are often ignored in the community because of their undesirability (Kirk and Therrien, 1975) and because of the lack of facilities to treat them. To the public these ex-patients appear as a nuisance and a burden on society; brought closer to the real world they have only increased fears and hostilities because usually they are grouped together in neighbourhoods and are seen as a threat to normal life. Former patients of mental hospitals are not welcomed back into communities with open arms, they are often confronted by formal and informal attempts to exclude them from the community by using city ordinances, zoning codes and police arrests (Kirk and Therrien,

1975). Actual residence in 'the community' can be just as disabling, frightening, dehumanising, and isolating as living in the back wards of more formally structured institutions (Kirk and Therrien, 1975).

The problem is not confined to the USA: the increasing numbers of elderly in Britain (and indeed elsewhere) has created specific needs that the statutory caring services cannot meet. At the beginning of the century life expectation in Britain was 48 years for men and 52 years for women. Now it is 72 and 77 years respectively. In 1901 only 1 person in 20 was in the age group 65+ for men, and 60+ for women; today it is almost 1 in 5 (Johnson, 1988). Over the six-year period from 1980 to 1985 the population of Great Britain aged 65 and over rose by 1.7 per cent; those over the age of 75 increased by 13.4 per cent and those over the age of 85 years by 17.8 per cent (HMSO, 1987b). The Government Actuary Department forecasts that by 1988 there will be 715 000 more people in the 75–84 age group than in 1974 and an additional 450 000 over the age of 85 years (HMSO, 1986B).

On current demographic trends, given expected advances in medico-biological research to control the major causes of premature death (heart disease and cancers in particular) along with a better diet, life styles, housing and work conditions, by 2050 living to 130 is a reasonable prediction (Johnson, 1988) for those living in the Western world. Depression is a endemic condition, whilst dementia of the Alzheimer's type will affect between 5 per cent and 15 per cent of people of 75 years and over (Johnson, 1988).

This increase in the numbers of elderly has occurred at a time when the old geriatric/psycho-geriatric hospitals and wards are gradually being phased out. Far more people are now being treated for acute illnesses, which means a higher turnover and greater bed usage. There has been a reduction in the average length of stay of NHS patients by almost 50 per cent from 94 to 48 days. Much is being achieved, it would seem, by intensive rehabilitation programmes and a multidisciplinary approach.

The reality however, is, quite different. There is no money available for the long-term back-up facilities needed for the elderly who may very well have benefited from a 'short sharp dose of hospital treatment'. Jones found that in nearly all the cases of patients discharged to the community, that she studied, the Department of Health and Social Services did offer some form of help, but it tended to tail off after some time. The only consistent help came from day centres and MIND. Social workers and community psychiatric nurses called a few times and then ceased to come when patients were thought to be no longer in need of regular support (Jones, 1985). Nursing care for the chronically sick, who cannot be helped by surgery or rehabilitation does and will remain a low priority for NHS resources because it is unfashionable and unprestigious (Holmes and Johnson, 1988).

The response to this problem has been swift, through necessity. The intense pressure on the modern treatment-focused services of the NHS has meant that people are often discharged prematurely from hospital into a community which is not set up to cope with them. Many people who might well have become long-stay hospital patients now have no choice but to turn to whatever else is available to them. The choice is currently simple – rely on relatives to provide them with 24-hours-a-day care or turn to the private nursing homes that are springing up everywhere. The problem – in a society where jobs are scarce, geographical mobility is high and the need for women to work has gently increased – may very well be that there is no choice.

Private residential care

Private residential care for elderly people in Britain, and especially elderly people with mental health problems, expanded steadily in the 1970s and more dramatically from the 1980s onwards. In 1974 19 283 people over the age of 65 years lived in private rest homes in England and Wales. By 1979 this had risen to 26 840 and five years later in 1984 the figure had doubled to 55 005 places. Private nursing homes which offer qualified medical supervision for those people who need it, followed the same pattern. In 1979 there had only been 13 000 occupied beds in private nursing homes, by 1984 there were 24 100 (HMSO, 1986B). By 1984 85 000 elderly people lived in private residential homes and a projection to the year 1990 showed a rise of 129 000 people in private and residential homes (Laing and Buisson, 1985).

The discharge of patients from mental hospitals, especially the older asylum types, has meant the mass discharge of elderly long-stay patients with chronic mental-health problems. This has increased the financial pressures on Local Authorities for whom this action by the Government has meant the transfer of responsibilities for community care from the underfunded National Health Service to local government, without adequate financial compensation. It has meant an actual decrease in provision by Local Authorities at a time when the need to provide more Local Authority Part III Accommodation was vital. The joint finance policies that were introduced in 1976 were intended to allow Local & Health Authorities to plan and jointly fund projects to replace the long-stay care and eventually to allow Local Authorities to take on the largest proportion of the costs. This has happened in some parts of Britain, but the pressure upon Local Authority budgets over the years has meant that funds intended for these budgets have been channelled back into the general coffers in order to maintain the existing essential health services (Holmes and Johnson, 1988).

Meanwhile, the growth in private homes continues, and little is known about such places. Whilst relatives have a choice between keeping their mentally ill elderly relative at home and sending them to a private nursing home, these homes have the right to refuse aggressive, disruptive or incontinent patients. This means that public homes are likely to have to take the more difficult patients. Jones found that Local Authority Homes staff – although for the most part kind, willing and hardworking – were not trained to care for confused or disruptive residents. They appeared to have little understanding of their needs, and were often worried about their own lack of training (Jones, 1985).

What of the costs involved in private nursing care? At the time of writing (1991) the Government allows an elderly person £200.05p per week through DSS grants to pay for nursing-home care. The average place in a nursing home costs around £210 per week (in 1991) and with fees rising to compensate for the newly introduced Community Charge (known as the Poll Tax), this might appear somewhat of a conservative estimate. These fees usually exclude such things as personal effects, clothing and services like chiropody (often essential to the elderly). The difference between the Government allowance and the costs involved have to be met from savings and if none exist, through relative subsidising the difference, for it is the relatives who sign the contract with the nursing homes. Where there are no savings and no relatives the private nursing homes at present can choose whether to keep them or not. Security in retirement in the early 1990s is seemingly a thing of the past.

Local authority Part III accommodation

'Part III accommodation' is jargon for 'accommodation provided by local government or local authorities'. Nationally, places in Local Authority Residential Homes in England and Wales rose slowly from 98 634 in 1974 to 109 117 in 1979 and remained fairly constant up to and including 1984 (109 082 places). Changes in the method of calculating the level of pensions, and supplementary benefits working alongside the extremely complicated Housing Benefit Scheme, have affected both the level of incomes of pensioners and their ability to obtain their rightful entitlement. Similarly, in the USA the great complexity of the Social Security set-up has resulted in the poor levels of accommodation and psychiatric treatment available to people with mental health problems particularly those who are also old. Estimates of the numbers of homeless in New York City have placed them as high as 36 000; parks and transportation terminals and other public spaces are paid to have become less comfortable because of discharged patients loitering there (Brown, 1985).

In Britain the National Audit Office (NAO) noted that the 1980 Social Security Act resulted in a growing awareness by Local Authorities and the public, that residents in private and voluntary homes could claim supplementary benefit. This had some interesting effects. First, between 1980 and 1983 the number of elderly residents in private and state run homes which were sponsored by Local Authorities fell by 22 per cent from 18 729 to 14 558. Second, the number of elderly residents in private and voluntary homes who were receiving supplementary benefit increased by 104 per cent from 11 558 to 23 577. The DHSS observed that the amount of benefits paid to all residents in such homes showed an increase of 483 per cent from £18 million at December 1980 to £105 million at December 1983 (HMSO, 1987).

The results have been quite remarkable as the NAO have reported. Whilst the percentage change of residents in Part III Local Authority Homes was a 0.9 per cent decrease, and in Local-Authority-sponsored homes a 45 per cent decrease, private nursing and voluntary home places had increased by 115.9 per cent.

Data for the South-East Thames Region showed gross deficiencies in both the NHS and Local Authority provision for psychiatric services; the problem being more serious for psychiatric patients (Brough and Watson, 1977).

The changing structural position of psychiatry

Of major importance to the 'care' of those with mental-health problems is the role of psychiatry, or more specifically that of psychiatrists. For if the 'care' is to be delivered in the community, the psychiatrists must also move away from the mental hospitals, whilst at the same time keeping the link with in-patient facilities. Unless in-patient treatment disappears altogether, the psychiatrist must work within both the community and the hospital, thus maintaining a balance between the two. Currently, in the early stages of community care in Britain, psychiatrists are finding themselves working within the old mental asylums, as well as in new units attached to general hospitals, and holding sessions in health centres and general practitioners' surgeries, and, in some more advanced cases, in their own bases.

Psychiatrists are now 'specialists' working alongside general practitioners, giving advice and training about the diagnosis of mental-health problems, whilst they also have similar status to surgeons and physicians within the general hospitals (Bean and Mounser, 1989).

At the same time the auxiliary staff, such as the community psychiatric nurses, the social workers, the psychologists and the occupational therapists, have also left the hospital and are now working within the community. Their responsibilities have undergone subtle changes from those traditional ones within the hospital. Sometimes patients only see auxiliary staff, as psychiatrists are prepared more and more to hand patients over at allocation meetings. This is justified by the philosophy of community care, where some people with suspected mental-health problems are seen to have 'social' rather than 'medical' problems. Working within general practice means that general practitioners are able to refer patients directly to the auxiliary staff, especially if their problems are not medical. The auxiliary staff come more and more to be assessors of patients, making decisions about whether patients ought to be seen by a psychiatrist or whether they can remain under auxiliary care. In a system where community care is well-established, as in Nottingham, where psychiatric care has been delivered in the community since 1984 (and other features as early as 1981), it is not uncommon for auxiliary staff to act as referral agents, referring patients to hospital themselves (see Chapter 4: Sectorisation and social control – the alternative to the mental hospital). If a patient has been seen solely by a social worker attached to a community team, and the social worker feels the patient is ill enough to need hospital treatment, that patient might find himself in a mental illness unit without actually ever having seen a psychiatrist. And what is also happening is that the links with the mental hospital and mental illness units in this kind of system have become extended to include the multidisciplinary team who, together with the psychiatrists, offer the alternative to the mental hospital.

4
Sectorisation and Social Control: The Alternative to the Mental Hospital

Some of the general characteristics in the shift of patient care from the hospital to the community were described in Chapter 3. We will now be more specific and outline the setting in which patients receive treatment. The modern system which we describe is called *sectorisation*. Under this system patients are treated by community psychiatric teams. Treatment is mainly conducted in the community, but patients are transferred to the hospital, if required. It is the community teams who will look after the patients in hospital and again when they return to the community. This provides continuity of treatment and care. (At least this is what is supposed to happen.) The teams are organised in sectors taking responsibility for a population of about 100 000 people per sector. In this chapter we shall look at the way patients are referred to different parts of the system, showing how and when they leave hospital and the part the hospital plays in the process – including the impact that recent mental health legislation has had on patient care.

Sectorisation – a model of a community care programme

'Sectorisation' extends the care of the patient into the community i.e. a patient will have the same consultant in hospital as in the community and this implies that the care is continuous and under the control of the consultant. 'Sectorisation' by itself is not a system of 'community care', but the administrative means by which it can be achieved. Strictly speaking sectorisation merely defines the way in which the district is divided up into roughly equal portions or sectors. As the system applies in Britain and as a general rule each sector has two consultant psychiatrists allocated to it, each with a multidisciplinary team of workers who are

64

responsible for a population of approximately 100 000 people. Whereas in the hospital-based system a psychiatrist would be expected to criss-cross the district when s/he was on duty visiting patients wherever they might be, now s/he is confined to one sector and deals with those patients whether as in-patients or out-patients within that sector. However, within this sectorised system not all psychiatrists operate this way; those who are specialised – e.g. offer an alcohol and drug service, or rehabilitation, or psychotherapy – still cover the whole of the district and take patients wherever they might live. Not all the specialists are totally hospital-based, however, for some are beginning, through their own multidisciplinary teams, to move out into the community (see also Bean and Mounser, 1989).

The origins of this new concept of care lie deep within the history of psychiatry, but especially in the mid-nineteenth-century. With the 'modern age' of psychiatry came new categories of pathology notably the concept of 'neuroses', which would have been severe enough to warrant hospitalisation. Armstrong (1980) provides us with a detailed account of how the concept of neurosis has been exploited to provide the main disorders of the non-hospitalised population and has enabled psychiatrists to venture out into the community. New venues for intervention become established in which psychiatry can attack pathology at its very roots – family life, industry and the school system. New specialities can then develop which are based on the medical model and come within psychiatric jurisdiction e.g. clinical and educational psychology, psychoanalysis, criminology and social work combine to facilitate expansion (Ingleby, 1983).

In this way the modern multidisciplinary team was forged. That type of team would cover a wide variety of disciplines. Under sectorisation each team consists of a consultant psychiatrist, two doctors at the registrar level, and varying numbers of social workers, community psychiatric nurses, psychologists, and occupational therapists depending upon the emphasis of each team which is at the discretion of the consultant psychiatrist. Using the Nottingham experiences, which is the most advanced in Britain and probably as advanced as anywhere, sectorisation consists of six sectors and seven specialities. The total number of allied community psychiatric nurses is 78 and there are 57 occupational therapists in total, and four physiotherapists. The system operates around the allocation meeting where patients are allocated to individual members of the multidisciplinary team according to their individual needs; if for example, their problems, are considered to be social they will be allocated to a social worker and so forth.

Each team operates from a different base, some remaining within the hospital and going out into the community, while others have sector bases or hold clinics in general practice surgeries or health centres, thus developing strong links with the community through the general practitioners (GPs).

Sectorisation in its advanced stages has led to the sectorised psychiatric teams in ways that are substantially different from traditional modes of operation. Whereas in the past the consultant psychiatrist and his junior doctors worked within and from the hospital, now the expanded multidisciplinary teams operate within the community. The community is the new treatment arena and the hospital has become the back-up facility, the place where patients are now admitted when they can no longer be contained in the community. It would be assumed, therefore, that over time the use of the hospital as the main treatment arena would decline, especially as seen in Nottingham where a visible decrease in hospital populations is observed and exemplified by its decreasing admission rate.

There are very few research studies which look at the way sectorisation works. As Nottingham has pioneered sectorisation we have chosen this city to describe in some detail the key features of sectorisation and show some of the implications for practice. We are not claiming that Nottingham is representative of other cities who have chosen to introduce sectorisation; we have presented our data in the hope that later studies, and studies from countries other than England and Wales can use the material for comparison.

Sectorisation at work in Nottingham

Admissions

Table 4.1 shows all admissions to mental hospitals in the Greater Nottingham area between 1978 and 1985. The figures show a gradual reduction in admissions which on the face of its supports the assumption that the hospital is in a decline as a major treatment arena – the table shows a net reduction of about 200 patients from 1405 to 1222.

Table 4.1   *All admissions of patients*
15 years and over to Greater
Nottingham mental hospitals*
between 1978 and 1985

Year	Admissions
1978	1405
1979	1372
1980	1400
1981	1293
1982	1230
1983	1238
1984	1206
1985	1222

* This table excludes the now non-existent
Saxondale Hospital.

Source: Nottingham Psychiatric Case
Register, Bulletin No 3, September 1987.

Readmissions

However, if we look more closely we shall see that the matter is
more complicated. Crude admission figures mask other changes.
The most important feature is that whilst the admission rate declined, the readmission rate has increased over the same period.
This phenomenon can be best observed by looking at the number
of patients who were admitted for the first time in each year i.e.
called life-time first admissions, compared with those patients
who had subsequent admissions in each year i.e. readmissions).
Table 4.2 gives the data for patients aged 15–64 who were admitted as emergencies. Those patients who were 65 years and over
have been excluded as they were dealt with quite differently in
this community-based service.

It can be seen that whilst the numbers of new patients have
reduced from 477 to 278 over the nine-year period, readmissions
have, in fact, increased; although it must be said that the readmission rate is not sufficient to overcome the decline in the overall
admission rate. Even so this change in the readmission rate has an
important bearing on the way community psychiatry works, for it
shows how patients are transferred from one part of the system to

Table 4.2   *Patients aged 15–64 admitted to Greater Nottingham mental
hospitals* between 1977 and 1985 and the number of formal
admissions*

Year	Life-time first admissions	Formal	%	Readmission	Formal	%
1977	477	52	(11)	234	37	(16)
1978	424	51	(12)	284	42	(15)
1979	393	50	(13)	335	50	(15)
1980	365	52	(14)	338	50	(15)
1981	345	53	(15)	340	71	(21)
1982	317	68	(21)	335	74	(22)
1983	311	52	(17)	329	91	(28)
1984	308	57	(19)	334	78	(23)
1985	278	48	(17)	364	82	(23)

* This table excludes the non non-existent Saxondale Hospital.

Source: *Nottingham Psychiatric Case Register*, Bulletin No 2, June 1987.

another. This point will be more fully explored later when we talk
of the patients' eventual discharge from psychiatric treatment and
the problems inherent in that: at this stage we wish to reassert a
more general point about the high numbers of readmissions going into the hospital system.

Patients leaving hospital

We wanted to know what happened to patients when they left
hospital, where they went, and what were their subsequent contacts with the community services. Sectorisation, if it means anything, will, or should, reintegrate the patient with the community
through the sector services. The community, as we have said
before, is the new treatment arena, the hospital is the backup
facility. We wanted to see what this mean for the various patients,
how they fared in the community, and what this transfer from
hospital meant?

Two areas of patient transfer can be identified: first, those
leaving hospital whilst 'under a section', and, second, those leaving hospital generally. The former is rather less important for the
number is small but it shows up some of the new legal provisions
and methods used to deal with them. It also ties in with the

chapter on Community Treatment Orders. The latter feature will be dealt with in more detail.

Leaving hospital 'on a section'

Section 17 of the Mental Health Act 1983 allows leave of absence from hospital to patients who are detained on a section of the Act: 'Leave of absence may be granted to a patient under this section either indefinitely or on specified occasions or for any specified period; and where leave is so granted for a specified period, that period may be extended by further leave granted in the absence of the patient' (Section 17(2)). However, leave of absence can be terminated and the patient brought back into hospital if the responsible medical officer thinks it is in the interests of the patient's health or safety or for the protection of others to do so (section 17(5)). After six months' absence the patient is no longer liable under any section. A patient can, therefore, be discharged on a section 2 (the 28-day assessment order) or a section 3 (the treatment order), or a section 37 (court order; either with section 41 restrictions or without), subject to recall by use of section 17.

The point of holding a patient in hospital under section 2, 3 or 37/41 of the Act, we can see, is that in the opinion of a psychiatrist the patient who is detained needs to be in hospital for either assessment or treatment. To discharge someone for a trial period, using the new community assessment arrangements, as previously described, to allow the multidisciplinary team the opportunity to assess a patient in their own homes, seems to us in some cases to benefit the patient, or at least to have the potential to do so. However, to discharge someone, subject to recall as a practice, seems only to benefit those who are administratively liable to operate the Act with minimum paper work. The only other explanation, we believe, is that doctors are possibly no longer sure when a patient is ready to be returned to the community. If they were sure, we feel, they would not need to keep patients on hospital orders when they return them to the community.

In 1986 in Nottingham 72 (or 25 per cent) of the 284 patients who were detained under the 1983 Mental Health Act were discharged still under a section of the Act. 44 of the 72 patients (or 61 per cent) discharged on a Section were discharged under section 17 of the Act. Of the 44 patients discharged subject to recall, 10 were in fact recalled. The sections on which the patients were discharged were: 29 patients (40.3 per cent) discharged on Section

2 (the 28-day assessment order), 39 (54.2 per cent) on section 3 (6 months' treatment order) and 4 patients (5.6 per cent) on a section 37/41 (section 37 empowers the courts to place a person on guardianship in hospital and section 41 restricts discharge from hospital).

39 per cent of those who left hospital on a section (or 28 patients) were not subject to recall; this means that they were not placed on leave of absence, but left with some of their section still left to run. Although in practice this does not contravene the Act, it means that these patients were being treated as if they were subject to recall. The possible explanations of leaving patients on sections are many, notably:

1. to be able to bring patients back into hospital, as if they were subject to recall, if the doctor thinks it appropriate that they cannot settle in the community (it must be remembered that in a community-based system the same team of doctors etc. will treat the patient in the community as well as in the hospital);
2. to avoid the administration of discharging the section, and later finding the patient needs readmitting, and formally;
3. since the implementation of the Mental Health Act 1983 more responsibilities have been placed upon hospital managers to provide whatever information is relevant, not only to the patients detained under the various provisions of the Act, but also to their relatives. This, it has been shown, places excessive administrative burdens on current staff who have not been given additional resources for such a task (Davis and Tutt, 1983). The increased use of sectioning may have added to this problem.
4. because they have been overlooked. In a system such as that used in Nottingham, where handwritten rather than computerised records are kept for work under the Mental Health Act, and where each section is recorded in a separate ledger, it is often easy to overlook the progress individual patients make from formal to informal status and so on (48.9 per cent of the patients in Nottingham in 1986 were regraded two or more times and one patient as many as seven times during the course of one admission);
5. to maintain the same level of compliance from the patient that they received in hospital, i.e. the extension of hospital orders to the community.

We wondered at the logic behind placing one of these patients on a 28-day assessment order, and then sending the patient out of hospital after only two days. Did this patient, in fact, need to be placed on an order at all? And, indeed, did the patient need to be in hospital? Furthermore, the practice of bringing patients back into hospital in order to extend the period of the section, is technically illegal, yet has not ceased to operate (see Chapter 5 for a more detailed discussion on Community Treatment Orders and patients discharged on leave).

Leaving hospital generally

Before looking more closely at some of the data relating to patients leaving hospitals, some comments are required, to set the scene, and show how the new system should operate.

The discharge procedure under the new regime is no longer a simple process of leaving the institution and returning to the community. With the psychiatrist and the multidisciplinary team now operating in the community there has developed the opportunity of assessing patients in their own homes in order to see if they can cope; in the past this was called trial leave. Whereas trial leave was a period in which the patient spent a short time at home to see if s/he could cope, the assessment of ability to cope was left very much to the patient and his/her family; the new system allows the psychiatrist and/or member of the multidisciplinary team to perform this function. Often the psychiatrist will visit the patient at home and so be able to assess the patient together with his/her social circumstances, and his/her behaviour in relation to other members of the family. It is becoming quite common, under this community-based psychiatric service, for a community psychiatric nurse to spend a whole day at home with a patient in order to assess him/her. If the nurse decides that the patient is not ready to return home on a full-time basis the nurse will refer the patient back to the hospital. As far as the hospital is concerned, the patient's bed has been kept in readiness for such an instance. Sometimes the patient may spend a few weeks at home before s/he is officially recorded as discharged.

The concept of 'discharge' has, therefore, undertaken a subtle change. In an institutionally-based system it means the releasing of the patient from hospital care, to be returned to the community. In a community-based system a patient may not be discharged but may be living within the community, and at times still be subject to the rules and conditions that operate within the hospital.

Yet in neither case is discharge clearly related to the cessation of contact with a psychiatrist. In an institutionally-based system discharge from hospital may mean follow-up by the psychiatrist in an out-patient clinic, or the patient may attend an injection clinic, or even an ECT (electro-convulsive therapy) clinic. In a community-based system follow-up may be in the patient's home, a general practitioners' (GP) surgery or in a sector-based out-patient clinic, as well as the more traditional arrangement of hospital-based clinics. In both instances follow-up might be by a social worker, although in a hospital-based system this will be largely related to the discharge and the resettlement back into the community, after which contact may cease. Any one member of the multidisciplinary team may be the follow-up agent, and it is quite common for the community psychiatric nurse to take over supervision of injections in the patient's home.

The whole concept of the discharge from hospital has clearly changed. There is now a great blurring of the demarcation lines between the hospital and the community. This can be seen in the use of the Mental Health Act which, apart from Guardianship Orders, is traditionally and legally applied to the hospital setting alone. It is in this area that a blurring has occurred and the temptation to transfer the use of the Mental Health Act, as if it were applicable to the community, becomes too great.

Turning now to the patients themselves: our data applies to all patients leaving the Nottingham Mental Hospital over a two year period. It allows us to follow up patients and see what happens to them when they return to the community: in this way we are able to show that the community is now the new treatment arena.[1]

In the years 1985 and 1986 there were 1825 and 1744 patients discharged respectively. All were followed up for a significant period. Table 4.3 gives the details of the length of stay in hospital before discharge.

Table 4.3 shows the most usual length of stay to be between 1 and 2 months but with over half staying less than one month (57 per cent for 1985 and 55.6 per cent for 1986). Whatever else the modern system of psychiatry has achieved it has led to a reduction in length of stay in hospital. A decade or so ago patients could have expected to stay 3 months or more, and in the 1960s longer still. How much of the change can be directly attributable to the decarceration movement is difficult to say. We believe, and

Table 4.3 *Length of stay in hospital before discharge in 1985 and 1986*

Length of stay	1985 Frequency	%	1986 Frequency	%
< 1 week	280	15.2	243	13.8
1 – 2 weeks	344	18.8	305	17.5
2 – 4 weeks	418	22.9	425	24.4
1 – 2 months	488	26.7	498	28.6
2 – 6 months	210	11.5	180	10.3
6 – 12 months	36	2.0	33	1.9
12 months – 3 years	23	1.3	25	1.4
3 – 5 years	7	0.4	5	0.3
5 – 15 years	12	0.7	15	0.9
15 years plus	7	0.4	15	0.9
	1825	100.0	1744	100.0

$X^2 = 6.9$; $df = 7$; $p < 0.5$ not significant.

our anecdotal evidence supports this, that length of stay has been shortened by a new philosophy which is eager to get the patient back into the community as soon as possible, but changes in forms and types of treatments which preceded this have helped also. Table 4.3 gives a remarkably even picture over the two years (the X^2 value is low, at 6.9 and $p < 0.5$ not significant) except that rather more long-stay patients were discharged in 1986 than 1985, i.e. 'long-stay' is defined as a stay of over 1 year and there were 60 in 1986 compared with 49 in 1985, but this was not a significant difference).

Again the data show similar distribution whether by sex or age, in each year. Neither table gives data which is significantly different over the years (Table 4.4 $p < 0.8$ and 4.5 $p < 0.2$ not significant), yet Table 4.5 shows rather more patients discharged in the 65+ age group in 1986 than in 1985 (593 or 34.0 per cent as opposed to 571 or 31.3 per cent). Apart from a slight discrepancy in the 45–54 age group the aggregate and percentages remain remarkably similar throughout.

Table 4.6 provides the data for diagnosis – that is, the diagnosis given to the patient before they left the hospital.

As with the other tables the pattern of diagnosis remains fairly even over the two years – though perhaps rather less so than with the other data. (The level of probability is different but still not significant). Aside from the category, 'other', the category, 'affec-

Table 4.4   *Relative numbers of male and female patients discharged from mental hospitals in 1985 and 1986*

	1985	1986	Total	%
Male	812	783	1595	44.7
Female	1013	961	1974	55.3
Total	1825	1744	3569	100.0

$X^2 = 0.04$; $df = 1$; $p < 0.8$ not significant.

Table 4.5   *Relative numbers of patients in different age groups discharged from mental hospitals in 1985 and 1986*

	1985 Frequency	%	1986 Frequency	%
15–24	125	6.8	118	6.8
25–34	295	16.2	304	17.4
35–44	305	16.7	288	16.5
45–54	245	13.4	186	10.7
55–64	284	15.6	255	14.6
65+	571	31.3	593	34.0
Total	1825	100.0	1744	100.0

$X^2 = 8.96$; $df = 5$; $p < 0.2$.

Table 4.6   *Diagnoses of patients discharged in 1985 and 1986*

	1985 Frequency	%	1986 Frequency	%
Organic	198	10.8	219	12.6
Schizophrenia	270	14.8	285	16.3
Affective psychosis	367	20.1	304	17.4
Neurotic	284	15.6	281	16.2
Alcohol and drug addiction	177	9.7	187	10.7
Others	529	29.0	468	26.8
Total	1825	100.0	1744	100.0

$X^2 = 9.29$; $df = 5$; $p < 0.1$ not significant.

tive psychosis', is the largest group, followed by those suffering from 'neurosis', then those with schizophrenia, then organic and finally alcohol and drug addiction – this although the smallest is nonetheless large by national standards, reflecting the specialist interest of one psychiatrist at the Nottingham Hospital.

Next, where did the patients go when they left the hospital? The data in Table 4.7 show that most went home, with a few going to Part III accommodation and private nursing homes. Most returned to the community – presumably from whence they came.

To summarise so far: the modal patients would have been in hospital for a short period of time, were more likely to be women than men, would be in the 65+ age group, be suffering from affective psychosis and would be discharged back home. We now wish to take the argument further to see what happened to these and other types of patients. We followed them up over a period of 6 months from being sent out of hospital. The data were taken from the hospital records.

We were concerned first to count, then later provide a more detailed examination of post-discharge contacts. We defined 'contacts' as occurring where patients had been to certain specified clinics such as those providing depot neuroleptic injections or ECT or where they had been seen by sector social workers or received liaison contacts through (Accident & Emergency) referrals, or where they had been seen by psychiatrists during a domiciliary visit, or had even been readmitted to mental hospital. The information on post-discharge contacts for both years is found in Table 4.8.

Table 4.7 *Destination of patients leaving hospital in 1985 and 1986*

Destination	1985 Frequency	%	1986 Frequency	%
Home	1580	86.6	1390	79.7
Part III accommodation (Local Authority Care)	109	6.0	82	4.7
Hostel	69	3.7	55	3.2
Private nursing home	60	3.2	107	6.1
Other hospital	–	–	41	2.3
No fixed abode	–	–	14	0.8
Other	7	0.5	55	3.2
Total	1825	100.0	1744	100.0

Table 4.8   *Number of contacts after discharge, 1985 and 1986*

| | 1985 | | 1986 | |
Value	Frequency	%	Frequency	%
No contact	650	35.6	688	39.4
One contact	352	19.3	323	18.5
2 – 5 contacts	620	34.0	596	34.2
6 – 10 contacts	174	9.5	109	6.3
10+ contacts	29	1.6	28	1.6
Total	1825	100.0	1744	100.0

$X^2 = 15.84$; $df = 4$; $p < 0.1$.

As with many of the other tables the data for Table 4.8 are similar throughout the two years – with the exception of the six-to-ten contacts which produced most of the X^2 value and the significant result. It showed a clear drop in 1986 from the 1985 figures. The data show that over half of all the patients discharged had no contact or only one in the 6-month follow-up period (54.9 per cent in 1985, 57.9 per cent in 1986), with a mean score of just three contacts per patient. At that simple and rather crude level we were left wondering if this could be what community care or sectorisation is supposed to be about, given the publicity, proclamations, statements of intent, etc., that preceded it. The average contacts work out at one every two months, with 35.6 per cent in 1985 and 39.4 per cent in 1986 having no contact at all.

We looked more closely at the type of contacts being offered. We found that out-patient appointments were the most favoured: 732 patients (or 40.1 per cent) had out-patients appointments in 1985 and 679 (or 38.2 per cent) in 1986. Next came readmission to the hospital, with 436 patients (or 23.4 per cent) readmitted in 1985 and 464 (or 26.6 per cent) in 1986. Other forms of contact occurred rather infrequently: for example, in 1985 only 67 patients had a domiciliary visit compared with 53 in 1986; 58 attended for injections in 1985 compared with 25 in 1986: 162 attended for social work contact in 1985, but this had dropped to 113 in 1986. Indeed the trend from 1985 to 1986 was for the patients to receive fewer of all types of contacts – as shown also in Table 4.8. Put simply at the aggregate level 'discharge' means what it has always meant – distance from treatment services with little follow-up.

We wanted to see if there were groups of patients who received rather more contacts – or community care services – than others and who was receiving the least. The first and obvious point to note from our data was that age was a significant factor in post-discharge contacts. Patients in the 15–24 age group received proportionately and significantly more contacts than those in the 65+ age group – in both years. (X^2 = 8.31 df = 1 p < 0.001 and in 1986 X^2 = 14.6 df = 1 p < 0.0001).

In 1986, for example, 43 per cent in the 15–24 age group had contacts compared with 25 per cent in the 65+ age group. Second, contacts were related to length of stay in hospital. Those staying the longest receiving the least number of contacts. In 1986 for example, only 1 person who had been in hospital over 3 years had two or more post-discharge contacts, and some who had been in over 10 years received none at all. (Most of these went direct to Part III accommodation exchanging the hospital for the old people's home and demonstrating that deinstitutionalisation sometimes means transinstitutionalisation.)

Not surprisingly, then, when we looked at the type of psychiatric condition and related this to patient contact, we found that those with an organic condition had the fewest (20.5 per cent in 1986), those with affective psychosis and schizophrenia rather more (52.9 per cent in 1986 for affective psychosis and 52.9 per cent in 1986 for schizophrenia). Table 4.9 gives the data for 1985 and 1986.

(The 'other' category includes, for 1986, 187 patients with a diagnosis of alcohol or drug addiction and 281 with personality disorders.)

Table 4.9 *Number of contacts and psychiatric condition on discharge for 1985 and 1986*

	Organic 1985–1986		Schizophrenia 1985–1986		Affective psychosis 1985–1986		Other 1985–1986		Total 1985–1986	
0–1 contacts	147	174	124	134	139	143	592	560	1002	1011
2+ contacts	51	45	146	151	228	161	398	376	823	733
Total	198	219	270	285	367	304	990	936	1825	1744

1985 X^2 = 100.1; df = 3; p < 0.001 significant.
1986 X^2 = 7.1; df = 3; p < 0.001 significant.

Our data show clear preferences in following-up these discharged patients. The groups least likely to receive contacts are the elderly, those suffering from an organic condition and those who had been in hospital the longest. Those receiving most contacts were the younger group, those who had had only short stay, and those suffering from schizophrenia or affective psychosis. We are left then with a clear impression of a service providing only a small number of post-discharge contacts generally, and then for specific groups of patients.

Interpreting the data

Our data show that 'community care' in the guise of the sectorisation of service provision, which at first seemed wonderfully progressive, turns out to be rather an anticlimax. (We have not of course considered patients who were dealt with by the community services but who did not enter hospital. Perhaps they were dealt with differently – more enthusiastically perhaps). The number of post-discharge contacts remains low. It also produced certain well-defined trends in patient care, with certain groups more favoured than others. At the admission stage there were also the new trends towards an increase in compulsory admission.

It is difficult to interpret these trends in a clear unequivocal way. Much has been said of the drift towards an increasing amount of psychiatric control, suggesting perhaps that inherent in the post-discharge phase is an increasing level of controls. This may well be true as far as the admissions are concerned – that is, with an increase in compulsory admissions and the use made of Section 5 – but not for patients who are discharged. If anything, some groups could see themselves as being neglected.

The data we have presented is not thought to be nationally representative of the workings of sectorisation – indeed it may be highly unrepresentative, given the way in which Nottingham has pioneered this type of community care. What it shows is that we should treat with scepticism some of the wilder claims being made that sectorisation is a panacea for most psychiatric ills. The reverse may be nearer the truth: that sectorisation creates new problems and recreates older ones: not least that it increases the use of compulsory powers as will be shown below. That we think is an important fact which should not be overlooked.

Compulsory powers and sectorisation

Turning next to the use of the compulsory powers the main point, as shown in Table 4.2, is that there has been an increase in the percentage of formal admissions, which is more marked for those patients who have had previous hospitalisation (i.e. for re-admissions). These increases raise questions about the use of compulsory powers in a community-based system, notably:

1. Is this form of psychiatric community care really working, or are patients being left without care until they become either a danger to themselves and/or others?
2. Does the policy of admitting patients for shorter periods of time mean that patients are being discharged too soon, and find themselves genuinely unable to cope in the community, thus needing numerous readmissions i.e. the revolving-door syndrome?
3. Is the increased use of section admissions and especially read-missions real, or an artifact of the way sections are being used in general in this system?

The Mental Health Act (apart from Guardianship orders) and Section 135/136 are used either to admit patients to a mental hospital compulsorily or to detain them in order to prevent them from leaving hospital. The criterion for admission and detention of patients to hospital is that they are suffering from mental illness, severe mental impairment, psychopathic disorder or mental impairment, and are considered a danger to themselves and/or to others. Therefore, the type of patient and the conditions of patients who are admitted or detained in hospital are governed by legislation, and this also includes many of the facilities available on discharge. 'Legislation may not dominate the psychiatrists world view, but it remains a potent influence' (Bean, 1980). It is legislation that not only regulates actions, but creates the ethos which legitimates the psychiatrists' position in respect of other professional groups and in society in general. It adds concreteness to occupational roles, it reinforces members' perceptions of their tasks, and it adds a measure of internal validity where areas of doubt may exist (Bean, 1980). However, it is important to separate the nature of the legislation from the way it is being operated. Those who operate the 1983 Mental Health Act may do so from the best of intentions and from a humanitarian concern for the welfare of the patient, but one should almost without exception view groups of people who have power with some suspicion, especially if such power has no external checks or verification. Similarly one should view those who claim to operate in others' best interests with scepticism, especially where decisions related to others' 'best interests' involves the loss of liberty, even if it is in a hospital.

That apart, the central question remains: does the Mental Health Act gradually become obsolete in a system where decarceration is the prime focus, or is it operated in an adaptable sense to fit the new system? Again, the operational model to be used will be that which exists in Nottingham where the Psychiatric Community Care policy is well-advanced and the closure of the last of its mental hospitals is imminent.

To understand more about what is happening it is important to look at the use made of section admissions, whether direct section detentions or the holding powers used to detain patients within the system.

Taking the year 1986 we looked at the use made of sections under the 1983 Mental Health Act. In all, 284 patients were admitted, detained or discharged under a section of the Act; in some cases we found certain patients to have numerous in-patient stays under compulsion during this year. Some were admitted informally and later (or the same day) held on a section 5.4 or 5.2, or under some other section of the Act (see below for a description of Section 5).

Patients may be admitted to hospital under several sections of the 1983 Mental Health Act. Those used the most are Section 2 and Section 3, the first an assessment order (but where treatment can be given) and the second a treatment order. Section 2 allows a 28-day assessment and treatment period on the grounds that the patient:

(a) is suffering from mental disorder of a nature or degree which warrants the detention of the patient in a hospital for assessment (or for assessment followed by medical treatment) for at least a limited period;

(b) ought to be so detained in the interests of his own health and safety or with a view to the protection of other persons.

Moreover, the assessment period should not exceed 28 days beginning with the day on which the patient was admitted. Section

3 allows the patient to be detained for treatment on the grounds that:

(a) he is suffering from mental illness, severe mental impairment, psychopathic disorder or mental impairment and his mental disorder is of a nature or degree which makes it appropriate to receive medical treatment in a hospital;
(b) in the case of psychopathic disorder or mental impairment, such treatment is likely to alleviate or prevent a deterioration of his condition;
(c) it is necessary for the health and safety of the patient or for the protection of other persons that he should receive such treatment and it cannot be provided unless he is detained under this section.

Of the 284 patients, 136 (or 47.9 per cent) were admitted on Section 2, 17 (or 8 per cent) on Section 3 and 95 (or 33.5 per cent) were admitted informally and sectioned later. Other section admissions included 18 section-4 admissions, which allows for admission for assessment in an emergency when delay in awaiting section 2 papers may be undesirable; and a very small number of section 135, used to remove people from public places. The one section-136 noted by the Nottingham Psychiatric Case Register was the only one recorded since the inception of the computerised Register in 1975. This is a reflection of locally developed forensic psychiatric services which are unique to Nottingham and the services relationship with the police, rather than an indication that the police are less likely to become involved with mentally ill people found in distressed states in public places (see also Bean *et al.*, 1991). Those people who might find themselves held by the police because they had been found distressed in a public place, could be referred to the forensic psychiatric service if necessary and admitted under the normal provisions of the Act.

These figures show that most patients were admitted for the 28-day assessment – nearly 50 per cent, rather less on Section 3 and relatively few on the emergency order. However, these figures on compulsory admissions provide a somewhat disturbing picture as the percentage and aggregate has increased. This has to be set against a national trend which began as far back as 1960 when the percentage of compulsory patients had steadily declined. Now it seems the trend is reversed, at least as far as Nottingham's community-based service is concerned. Might it not therefore be that sectorisation actually produces higher levels of compulsory admissions than hitherto? We shall return to the point in the last chapter.

If the number of compulsory admissions were not bad enough the figures for Section 5(2) – the so-called holding order – gives an even greater cause for concern. Section 5(2) relates to patients who are already in hospital, but where:

> it appears to the registered medical practitioner in charge of the treatment of the patient that an application ought to be made under this part of this Act for the admission of the patient to hospital, he may furnish to the managers a report in writing to the effect; and in any such case the patient may be detained in the hospital for a period of 72 hours from the time when the report is so furnished (HMSO, 1983a).

The application for 'admission' where a patient is already in hospital means a change to 'compulsory admission' from informal status. A Memorandum of the Act further states: 'An informal patient may also be detained for up to 72 hours under Section 5 if the doctor in charge of his treatment reports that an application for admission under Section 2 or 3 ought to be made' (HMSO Memorandum, 1983b).

Section 5(4) of the Act, which is generally used when Section 5(2) cannot be operated because there are no doctors available, allows a patient to be detained by a nurse:

> If, in the case of a patient who is receiving treatment for mental disorder as an in-patient in a hospital, it appears to a nurse of the prescribed class:
>
> (a) that the patient is suffering from mental disorder to such a degree that it is necessary for his health or safety or for the protection of others, for him to be immediately restrained from leaving the hospital, and
>
> (b) that it is not practicable to secure the immediate attendance of a practitioner for the purpose of furnishing a report under subsection (2) above.
>
> The nurse may record that fact in writing; and in that event the patient may be detained in the hospital for a period of six hours from the time when that fact is so recorded or until the earlier arrival at the place where the patient is detained of a practitioner having power to furnish a report under that subsection.

In fact, Section 5 of the Act is the only section that can be used by a non-psychiatrist in a non-psychiatric hospital (although this is rare); it can also be used on a patient who has had no previous psychiatric history:

> But where an in-patient is not receiving psychiatric treatment, the doctor who is in charge of the treatment the patient is receiving would have power to furnish the report. Where such a report is made by a non-psychiatrist, a senior psychiatrist should see the patient as soon as possible to determine whether the patient should be detained further (Memorandum of Parts I to VI, VIII and X of Mental Health Act 1983 (HMSOb).

What is curious about this part of the Act is that it allows non-psychiatric doctors to decide on the mental state of patients in general hospitals, and allows them to detain the patients. Although it recommends that a senior psychiatrist be consulted, it is not, in fact, for the purposes of confirming the action of the non-psychiatric doctor, but to decide whether the patient needs to be detained further.

Nationally the use of section 5(2) has fluctuated over the years, but between 1984 and 1985 showed a percentage reduction of 15.4 per cent (HMSO, 1987). However, there are no statistics related to the use of this section by non-psychiatric personnel. It was because of the observed increase in the use of section 5(2) in Nottingham, which has a community-based psychiatric service, that we became interested in its application. What seems to have happened since the 1983 Act came into being, and more specifically since the change-over to a community-based service, is that the use of section 5(2) has tripled. Not only this, but it has tripled on a greatly diminished hospital population, as demonstrated earlier.

In 1975 when the holding order under the 1959 Mental Health Act was section 30, there were 42 occasions when this section was used. Likewise, in 1982, prior to the 1983 Act, section 30 was used 59 times during that year. However, after the 1983 Act, when the holding order was changed to section 5, its use gradually began to increase. Certainly, our observations are that since sectorisation and the development of the community-based services in Nottingham, this section has become extremely popular – in 1985 it was used 85 times (including six section 5(4)s) in 1986 there were 87 (including eight section 5(4)s). By 1987 its use had increased to

132 (including twelve Section 5(4)s). Of course, an equivalent to section 5(4) did not exist in the 1959 Mental Health Act.

It was felt by many people involved in operating this section, whether clinically or administratively, that an increase in numbers reflected different ways of working. The prime concern, it appears, was to get the patient admitted as soon as possible; waiting for section papers to be completed in the community often kept the patients waiting, and their treatment was inevitably delayed because of the bureaucratic procedures. It was often easier then to get a patient into hospital and worry about the documentation later, therefore a section 5 holding order was used as a period of time in which to sort this out. Yet if this was so, and apart from the dubious legal practices involved, one would have expected any increase to lead to a decrease in the use of other sections such as Sections 2 or 3. Yet they have increased also.

It was interesting that clear differences existed between groups of patients detained under the various sections. Holding orders, i.e. Section 5, were almost always used for people who were admitted informally. For example, of the 95 patients admitted informally in 1986, 73 (or 96.1 per cent) were held under section 5(2); for only 3 other patients was section 5(2) used and these patients had been admitted under some other section initially. We were also curious to discover that in 51.6 per cent of cases section 5 was used on the same day as admission, with a further 10.9 per cent on the day after admission, which may have been less than 24 hours later depending upon time of admission.

We could not easily explain this except by reference to the point above: that the holding power was being used as a quick and easy way of detaining patients compulsorily which the Mental Health Act Commission holds is bad practice.

As previously stated, some people working within the hospital system felt that section 5 was being used as a way of bypassing the laborious red tape needed to get someone into hospital. Even if this were so, one would have at least expected that all those people placed on a section 5(2) (whether preceded by a 5(4) or not), would be later placed on a section 2 or section 3 at some time during the 72 hours they were being held; or certainly upon its expiration. Yet only half of the section 5(2)s were in fact being converted to another section. At the very least this seemed to us to contravene the spirit of the Act for section 5(2) can only operate as a holding order for the specific purpose of allowing a Section 2 or

3 to be made. But, as stated above, this occurred in only about 50 per cent of the cases in the Nottingham population.

We used Section 5 as an ideal type or test case to see how the system worked. When linked to some of the other data, especially on the increase in the numbers of compulsory admissions, in the readmissions group, we are led to conclude that community psychiatry, at least that practised under sectorisation in Nottingham, provides greater forms of psychiatric control. But is it endemic to the system or a by-product? We suspect the former: additional data on the use of Section 5 can be used to support our suspicion.

We looked at the source of referral for patients under Section 5; i.e. general practitioner's emergency domiciliary visit, social worker, etc. We found a situation that was puzzling. In only 30 of the 76 cases of patients held on Section 5(2) could it be established where they came from. Technically under sectorisation this cannot be so. No patients can be admitted to hospital without a previous contact, an out-patient appointment, a domiciliary visit, a contact in Accident and Emergency seen by liaison psychiatry etc.

That a patient could arrive on a psychiatric ward without a previous contact led us to speculate upon how this could happen. It seems that the possibility exists that all members of the multidisciplinary team are using the hospital as a back-up treatment arena. That is, social workers and community psychiatric nurses could be referring patients whom they are seeing directly to hospital where they are informally admitted and then held (on a section 5.4 or section 5.2) pending the psychiatric medical assessment. Incidentally, the applications made for the 5(2) sections were predominantly made by a junior doctor and not by the consultant. In fact in only 10.8 per cent of the cases was the application made by the consultant, the rest were by junior doctors except in one case where the papers had been mislaid and it remains unknown. Some of these patients may then subsequently be held formally on a section 2 or 3 and others are left until section 5(2) expires after 72 hours and are then discharged.

We suggest that social control is being extended to the wider group, the multidisciplinary team, who are gradually coming to have more and more powers in line with the medical model which they appear to emulate. The question that remains is, how is section 5 of the Mental Health Act being used in practice? If patients are being persuaded to come into hospital informally and over 50 per cent of them are being put on section 5(2) within 24 hours, how does the section appear to the patients? Is it being used:

1. pending the arrival of the section papers?
2. as an assessment period?
3. as a means of gaining cooperation to treatment?
4. inappropriately, where no section is sought?
5. as a means of stopping people from discharging themselves?

Some psychiatrists have said when asked how they use section 5(2), that it occasionally helps to gain cooperation from patients, at other times it allows section papers to be obtained. However, if a patient seems to settle down and become cooperative over this 3-day period, then often no further action is taken to place them on either a section 2 or a section 3. That is, we think it is being used as a trial period of compulsory detention. This, of course, was never intended by the Act, since it was specifically intended to be used in cases where a formal detention seemed appropriate. It would seem to us that if section 5(2) were not available so easily in this way, then psychiatrists would have to make decisions about detaining patients under an appropriate section of the Act. What seems also strikingly obvious is that if this section is being used as a trial period, then possibly junior doctors are not correctly assessing patients, thinking them to be in need of formal detention and, in fact, their senior doctor is overruling them – hence only 50 per cent of section 5(2)s are being converted.

When we looked at the socio-demographic features of the patients who were admitted, detained and discharged on section, there seemed to be very little difference between the groups. In all cases, as one would expect, the diagnoses of the patients were overwhelmingly schizophrenia, paranoid states and affective psychosis. The age and gender groups were much the same for all patients. In fact, we felt that this only reinforced our impression that the sudden and excessive use made of the Mental Health Act in this advanced decentralised service reflected on the one hand an increase in return to hospital of the more chronically ill patients who seemed unable to cope in the community and on the other hand a tendency on the part of the professional carers to try to use the Act as if it were applicable to the community. Some would argue that this is evidence of a need for a Community Treatment Order. Chapter 5 examines this concept in more detail.

5
Community Treatment Orders

Proposals for a Community treatment Order (CTO) are a logical extension of the move towards deinstitutionalisation and the treatment of patients in the community. They are directly relevant to the discussion about discharges of patients from mental hospitals because if implemented they would be expected to speed up the rate at which patients leave hospital. There are two main types of proposals on offer – one is confined to patients at the point at which they leave hospitals, another wants to go further, and extend CTOs to all patients, whether they have been in hospital or not. In both the aim is the same: to recreate hospital control systems in the community setting. This, of course, is part of the problem we have met before: how much further should treatment extend? Is the patient becoming enveloped in a control system from which it will be increasingly difficult to escape?

In an earlier chapter we described the working of the sector teams, and described the way in which patients were treated in the community. Here we wish to examine proposals for a new CTO as these proposals are a logical extension of sectorisation. At the time of writing (1991) the Government in England and Wales has not given its final decision on whether to introduce the CTO into British legislation. Yet whether introduced or not the proposals are interesting for they indicate the likely direction in which the debate is moving. Scotland, Canada and Israel are considering introducing CTOs whilst certain States of Australia and the USA have already introduced them (Task Force, 1987) when in this latter they are called out-patient commitment. Some American States have gone further and introduced preventative commitment. This involves placing a patient on an order, similar to a CTO but does not require the patient to have been in hospital. Its purpose is to prevent deterioration of a patient's mental condition so as to avoid in-patient commitment. In England and Wales there are no proposals as yet for preventative commitment, though some have come perilously close to being so. These proposals in

England and Wales tend to be restricted to in-patients and do not include out-patients who are not nor have been in hospital.

The justifications for a CTO

Briefly, supporters of the CTO have argued that a CTO would help to speed up or facilitate discharges from hospitals albeit for a limited number of patients – usually the chronic schizophrenics. As already mentioned, some proposals suggest that the CTO should be available for all mentally disordered patients irrespective of their current status, i.e. whether in hospital or not.) So, it is said, some discharged patients, being unable to function effectively in the community without medication, and without sufficient insight to see that they require treatment, could be assisted by a CTO. Claims are also made that a CTO would prolong the discharge period and so delay or perhaps avoid subsequent readmissions.

To give some idea about the sort of patient likely to qualify for a CTO, consider the following case history taken from an earlier research study (see Bean, 1980).

> A woman aged 35 was a single parent with two small children under 5 years of age. She had been discharged from the local mental hospital some 2 months earlier with instructions to maintain herself on medication to stabilise her schizophrenic condition. She had stopped taking her medication. Her earlier symptoms had returned and she and her children were in some distress. She was subsequently compulsorily admitted and the children taken into care.

Had there been a CTO, it is argued, the patient could have remained in the community and her children with her. The assumption here is that a compulsory order would somehow solve the patient's problem. But as we shall see later, having an order is one thing, solving problems is another.

Yet, whatever the merits of the proposal, the battle-lines are clearly drawn. It is no accident that those favouring the CTO have been those who would operate and enforce the order, i.e. psychiatrists, social workers and members of community psychiatric teams. Their powers would of course dramatically increase. Those against come from more disparate groups: mainly civil libertarians seeing the CTO as a further unwarranted threat to civil liberties and as another ill-advised extension of psychiatric controls. As with all battle-lines there remains the risk of overstatement and hyperbole, reawakening perhaps memories of earlier battles under different banners. Even so, the results or outcome of this battle are of some importance. Should the CTO ever become law in England and Wales it would be difficult to remove it.

Background to the current debate

Inevitably there have been, and will be, more than one type of proposal for a CTO – perhaps to be expected given the various pressure groups involved. There are also numerous positions taken up within those groups. Some in England and Wales have favoured a CTO run by Local Authority social workers, others by the psychiatric teams. Some want the CTO only for patients discharged from hospital – or as out-patient commitment; others would include out-patients who need not have been in hospital – i.e. what was earlier called preventative commitment. Others want an order equivalent to those provisions under Section 17 of the 1983 Mental Health Act whereby patients can be granted home leave, or conditional release. Still others want an extension of Guardianship. And so on and so on. Yet in spite of these numerous proposals there would, we think, be general agreement about the central justification of all these types of order. The CTO would require patients to receive prescribed treatment in the community where they would be supervised so as to make sure they took their treatment. The treatment itself might range from medication (including ECT) to counselling and job training. Similarly all justifications for the Order seem to be based on the view that there exist some patients who are unable to function effectively in the community without medication.

Before looking at some selected proposals for a CTO in England and Wales, one key question is: to what extent are CTOs effective? Much criticism could be stifled if CTOs were shown to take patients out of hospital and prevent their readmission. Such evidence as is available comes mainly from the USA. The difference in the psychiatric setting, including the use made of the Courts, makes interpretation difficult, but with this in mind there is some evidence available even if results are inconclusive.

RD Miller (1988) reports that in the USA as early as 1967, it was noted that *parens patriae* powers, under which most commitments to mental hospitals were made, would permit commitment to treatment in the community subject to the availability of resources. A small number of clinicians argued that the majority, if not all, of

patients traditionally hospitalised could be treated more effectively in the community. Miller goes on to say that the concept of
treatment in the least restrictive environment provided much of
the conceptual underpining to the debate (Miller 1985, 1988).

In England and Wales, the first set of formal proposals for a
CTO came from the British Association of Social Workers (BASW)
in a paper entitled *Mental Health Crisis Services: A New Philosophy*
(BASW, 1977). This sought to influence Government thinking at a
time when changes to the 1959 Mental Health Act were being
considered. BASW proposed a 'Community Care Order' (CCO)
whose aim would be 'to meet our aspirations to care for patients
in the least restrictive condition possible and within their own
living environment' (para. 4.2(i)). BASW recognised the changing
pattern of care from the hospital to the community and sought
to meet these changes. 'If the principle of care in the community
is to be properly pursued the present emphasis upon hospitalisation in the use of compulsory powers requires modification'
(BASW, 1977). BASW noted that an earlier Royal Commission
(the Percy Commission), provided a model and a precedent. That
Commissions' vision of care involved local authorities and private individuals accepting the responsibility for patients under
Guardianship.

> Local authorities as well as private individuals should be able to act as
> the guardian of mentally disordered patients who need community
> care, but for whom it cannot be provided without the use of compuls-
> ory powers. Their duty to arrange for the provision of community care
> should include a duty to accept the responsibility of Guardianship
> wherever Guardianship is appropriate and cannot otherwise be
> arranged (HMSO, 1957, para. 387).

It is difficult to see why BASW did not try to amend existing
provision for Guardianship, and proceed from there – or better
still, did not try to look more closely at what has been involved in
Guardianship before proposing something new. Yet it did neither. It simply asserted that Guardianship was not appropriate
and that there was a real need for some alternative to hospital
admission. But why? BASW did not say. However, in a later
paragraph entitled Guardianship Procedures, BASW saw the CTO
as 'superseding the existing powers of Guardianship'. BASW believed that there was a need for two orders: one, the traditional
Guardianship order which allows the Guardian to manage the
patient's property and affairs, deal with employment, perhaps

even accommodation, and up to the 1983 Act have powers over the patient equivalent to a parent having power over a child of less than 14 years of age; and second, the CTO 'which would provide compulsory powers to provide care within the community for use when the individual person refuses or is unable to agree with the recommendation that he is in need of such care' (BASW, 1977, para. 4).

BASW's failure to distinguish between a Guardianship Order and the proposed CTO, has bedevilled the debate from the outset. BASW assumed that Guardianship was not appropriate, yet for some unspecified reason suggested that the CTO would be. It implied that the CTO offered new thinking, (perhaps being more medically orientated than Guardianships), thus failing to acknowledge that Britain has had a compulsory care order of sorts for many years – called Guardianship and which has been rarely used. Moreover, BASW failed to ask specific questions about the working of a CTO. For example, would the CTO supervisor have more powers than the Guardian? Who would that supervisor be – a social worker, a relative, a psychiatrist or a community nurse perhaps? And given that Guardianship has been rarely used – there are only about 50 new cases of Guardianship in England and Wales each year (see Bean, 1986) – why should CTOs be used more often? Or, if only to put an earlier question in a slightly different way: if there is a need for such an order why not suggest improvements and modifications to Guardianship and leave matters there – as suggested by the Mental Health Act Commission? Clearly BASW had never seen Guardianship as attractive, or of value. It wanted a new order to provide new impetus – presumably on the basis that new structures are more appealing than revamped old ones.

Whether that is so or not a new order cannot escape its heritage – in this case the Guardianship order from which it is clearly derived and which it closely resembles. Guardianship was founded under the old Poor Law. Guardians were responsible for all who could not care for themselves: namely, children and people with mental disorders, including perhaps some elderly people. Guardianship was given its modern form under the 1913 Mental Deficiency Acts aimed at coping with mentally defective children as they were then called. Under the 1959 Act it was extended to include anyone with mental disorders, whether children or adults.

In this respect Guardianship was the forerunner and blueprint for the CTO. It represented a philosophy built around what the

Percy Commission called 'an integrated system between hospital and community' (HMSO, 1957, paras 466–8). The Commission saw Guardianship as involving care and control with patients transferring from hospital to the community. There was to be a corresponding blurring of the boundaries between the hospital and community – again devised and founded on the justification that Guardianship offered a less restrictive alternative to in-patient care. Patients on a Guardianship Order, said the Commission, should be transferred to hospital if necessary, and sometimes patients in hospital should be transferred to Guardianship – in the latter case for not more than 6 months after leaving hospital if proper care could not be guaranteed by other means. And in terms which are now familiar the Percy Commission said, 'Viewing the mental health services as a whole, hospital treatment should now be regarded as a stage which is commonly preceded and followed by some form of community care or out-patient treatment' (HMSO, 1957, para. 668).

Guardianship invokes that Victorian tradition of mixing care, cure and control, the emphasis shifting according to the needs of the patient. Guardianship also offers a low-cost form of care (though if undertaken properly it may turn out to be exceedingly expensive), and has the obvious appeal that it avoids in-patient care. Why then was it used so rarely? In their view of the 1959 Act the Government considered that the Guardian's powers were excessive (as a parent over a 14-year-old child). Under the 1983 Act it reduced them. Now the Guardian can no longer compel the patient to receive treatment though the patient can be compelled to attend for such treatment. Yet it still remains largely unused. Why? Perhaps because Local Authorities have always been reluctant to act as supervisors as Guardianship involves a long-term involvement with the patient. Incidentally Guardianship is viewed with suspicion by the Royal College of Psychiatrists as BASW's proposals would involve an order administered by local authority social workers. Support from the Royal College of Psychiatrists would be crucial if CTOs were to be successfully introduced – presumably only if they were run and supervised by the psychiatrists.

That support was indeed forthcoming. BASW's proposal might have gone no further but for the timely intervention of the High Court which put psychiatrists on the wrong side of two important High Court judgements, *Regina* v. *Hallstrom and Another ex parte W*, and *Regina* v. *Gardner and Another ex parte L.*, 1989. These High

Court judgements deal with what has been tastelessly described as the 'long-leash' procedure: that is, where compulsory patients could be discharged on home leave, returned to the hospital, usually for one night and so technically readmitted. They could then be discharged again. This allowed them to be placed again on a compulsory order for a further 6 months. Such practices provided a *de facto* CTO long before BASW suggested it – and, as we have described in Chapter 4, is a common practice under this new system of community treatments.

A full account of these judgements is given in the Notes of the book (*Law Reports*, 1986).[1] Briefly, *W*, and *L*. had been admitted to hospital on many previous occasions for treatment of their mental disorder. *W* was living in a hostel but refusing to take her medication. Her psychiatrist considered that she should be further admitted to hospital for treatment: she was admitted for one night and thereafter granted leave of absence (i.e. under Section 17, the Section which allows home leave to be granted) and returned to the hostel. *L* had also been granted leave of absence under Section 17 and was living at home. His responsible medical officer considered it was essential that he continue to take his medication but he was refusing it. He was recalled to the hospital at the end of his leave period, i.e. 6 months, with the intention of extending that leave. The High Court held that in these cases Section 17 was being unlawfully used to produce the effect of a long-term community treatment order; in one the intention being to extend the period during which a patient may be treated compulsorily in the community, in the other to retain the power of recall. This was not what the Act said and the Court ruled that the practice was unlawful.

The 'long-leash' procedures it seems, had, been widely used – and according to our data are still being used (see Chapter 4). The Mental Health Act Commission in its first biennial report, written before the Court judgements, noted that 'considerable use' was being made of the powers to grant conditional leave (this was the legal basis of the psychiatrists' powers which were challenged by the Divisional Court). The Commission too was wary of such use even though it had no powers to prevent it. It said, 'In some cases patients detention has been renewed . . . with the patient returning nominally to the hospital for that purpose, or sometimes not even returning at all: and in such an event the "long-leash" treatment continues beyond the 6 months of a detention under Section 3' (HMSO, 1985). The Commission saw an obvious link between

BASW's proposals for a CTO, the 'long leash' and the general move towards community care. It noted too the lack of facilities available:

> It seems likely that, with the reduction in hospitals beds, the greater use of hostels and group home accommodation, and the expansion of community psychiatric nursing services, the practice of using [this form of community treatment order] as a substitute for a community care order would become more widespread (HMSO, 1985, p. 26).

The Royal College of Psychiatrists reacted to the High Court judgements rather speedily. First it tried to insert into the Disabled Persons (Services Consultation Representation) Bill a clause which would allow for a community treatment order to be introduced. This was ingenious even if the chances of success were remote – and indeed the Royal College failed in this respect. (The Bill was aimed at providing for the improvement of the effectiveness of and the coordination of resources in the provision of services for people with mental and physical handicaps and for people with mental illness, to make further provision for the assessment of the needs of such people, and to establish from the consultation processes and representations rights for such people and for such persons (Parl Debates, *Hansard*, 4/12/85, vol. 88, cols 308–9).) The appropriate point for introducing such a measure as a CTO was in Clause 4 which dealt with consultation between health authorities and local authorities when the patient was discharged from hospital. Later in a letter dated 17 June 1986, to Mr John Clarke, an MP, the Royal College noted that 'the rundown of mental hospitals is already occurring up and down the country without adequate provision being made by local authorities' – or indeed by anyone else. The letter goes on to say 'In many areas there are no plans to accommodate vulnerable and dependent patients following their discharge into the community after many years in hospital (Hansard, 1986, vol. 89, col. 1350). The Royal College's solution was to propose a CTO. It did not appear to consider that such an order might be used as a justification for the Government to provide fewer community resources.[2]

The next step was for the Royal College to produce its own set of proposals under a discussion document entitled *Community Treatment Orders*. There are two such documents (Royal College of Psychiatrists, 1987, April 1987, and 23 October 1987). A third was promised but has not so far appeared (1991). The second document sets out the position in greater detail but essentially gives the same arguments: that is, there exists a group of patients usually described as suffering from chronic schizophrenia who are seen as being unable to function effectively in the community without periodic medication. These patients do not have sufficient insight into their condition to see that they need treatment. In the absence of compulsory treatment in the community these patients would be required to return to hospital and there remain under long-term compulsory detention. Using powers granted under a future CTO, such patients would be able to remain in the community. The Royal College talks of a CTO permitting medical treatment outside hospital where 'medical treatment' is defined to include 'nursing care, habilitation and rehabilitation under medical supervision'. The Royal College wanted procedures similar to those existing under Section 3 of the 1983 Act which permit compulsory detention in the hospital. The main criterion for the application of the order would be as with Section 3, i.e. that the patient requires compulsory treatment – 'except that for the CTO the treatment can be satisfactorily provided in the community rather than in hospital (Royal College of Psychiatrists, April 1987, para. 2).

These two discussion documents set out the Royal College of Psychiatrists' main proposals. Their stated aim is to meet the needs of a group of patients, the numbers of which are not given, who would otherwise be in hospital. The proposals are based on the belief that as community services expand it will be possible and indeed desirable to treat patients in the community (defined by the Mental Health Act Commission as including 'hostels, group homes and other forms of staffed or supervised accommodation'), especially those whose condition had hitherto required them to remain in hospital. The Royal College did not consider the possibility of patients who had not been in hospital being placed on a CTO. In this respect the proposal would not be expected to be used as a general supervision order for all classes of patients – unlike BASW's suggestion which seems to imply it should be more like a probation order available for all who need it.

Finally, in this overview of the various proposals for a CTO, there are the views of the Mental Health Act Commission to consider. The Commission in a discussion paper (1986) said that within its ranks there was no unanimity of view about imposing medical treatment upon people who no longer needed to be detained. It therefore set out arguments for and against compulsory treatment in the community. Those arguments in favour included the following:

1. that patients who would otherwise remain in hospital would be able to exist in the community if compulsion was provided;
2. that a CTO offers the patients the 'right to treatment', that is, patients who are ill often lack insight and the wherewithal to seek treatment. Moreover, an order compelling them to do so provides a 'duty to care' and would provide the necessary treatment.
3. there was justification for intervening and preventing people without insight from exposing themselves to a degenerative process without assistance, as occurs with the downward course of many psychotic conditions. Such treatment, said the Commission, offers a less restrictive alternative than compulsory treatment in a hospital;
4. that patients discharged on the 'long leash', albeit illegally, nevertheless benefited from the supervision;
5. that the Commission expected the current Government policy to continue: this meant further closure of long-stay beds in large psychiatric hospitals. A community alternative would therefore be required.

The Commission listed the following arguments against.

1. that the principle of personal autonomy is at the root of our democratic system and that there is a very heavy burden on those who argue for breaches against that autonomy;
2. that a CTO would enlarge the area of legal compulsion introducing and involving orders to a new class of mostly disordered patients in a manner that would be objectionable to civil libertarians;
3. that there were ethical dilemmas about forcing patients to take medication which may have unpleasant and disabling side effects and which may possibly not benefit them;
4. that there was the further objection relating to the moral justification for requiring someone to be symptom-free, i.e. forcing someone who is not acutely ill and taking away the freedom of choice of someone who can ostensibly manage a normal life in the community;

5. that there would be the protracted difficulty of ensuring compliance in the absence of any sanctions other than a compulsory return to hospital.

The Commission considered expanding existing provisions i.e. Guardianship (Mental Health Act Commission, 1986), but took the debate no further.

The Government has tended not to get involved though one of its Ministers said 'without prejudicing the discussion the Government would need to be very clear both of the benefits and that they would not be achieved through voluntary means before seriously considering asking Parliament to create provision for compulsory treatment in the community' (DHSS, Press Release, 13.7.89). A year later (May 1990) the Department of Health said it was willing to consider further representation about the desirability of amending the 1983 Act in order to introduce some form of CTO. Before proceeding however the Department said that it awaited another discussion paper from the Royal College – presumably meeting some of the criticisms made so far. It is not clear if and when a third Royal College paper will appear. Similarly the Mental Health Act Commission (through its Community Care Standing Committee) is also reconsidering the matter, but it too has no plans to produce a response unless required to do so – presumably at the Government's request.

The Royal College's proposals have attracted some support. Those in favour tend to be the more therapeutically inclined; they include social workers and of course psychiatrists, who would incidentally run the scheme and thereby acquire the greatest power. Support comes also from organisations such as the National Schizophrenia Fellowship, but not from the community psychiatric nurses (CPNs) who want nothing to do with it. This of course is a severe blow to the Royal College as the CPNs would have been expected to do the day-to-day supervision. Those opposed tend to be disparate groups of civil libertarians (and others of course) who see the CTO as another ill-advised proposal to extend psychiatric controls. As with all battle-lines there remains the risk of overstatement and hyperbole, reawakening perhaps memories of earlier battles under different banners. The results and outcome however are of some importance; should the CTO become law it will do more than set a precedent, it will create a new control system altogether.

We would like to look at a small number of key features of the CTO as proposed for England and Wales:

- Who would be on such an order?
- How would it operate?
- What would be the sanctions when the conditions were broken?

We begin with the types of patients for a CTO.

For whom would CTOs apply?

Who would be placed on such an order: would it be for discharge patients or others? Would it be for all patients satisfying certain criteria such as those with severe psychiatric conditions and perhaps being dangerous to themselves or others, (i.e. the same type of criteria covering compulsory admission generally?) Or would it only be for patients discharged from hospitals presumably operating similar to the so-called long-leash and using the same criteria as for section 3 of the 1983 Act. The Royal College of Psychiatrists appears to prefer this type of order – we say 'appears' because it is not always clear on this. Others, BASW for example, seem to view the CTO as a more general order, operating as a compulsory order in the community running parallel to in-patient orders. There are other differences between the Royal College and BASW. The Royal College wants the order to apply only to the mentally ill believing that other forms of mental disorder such as psychopathy, mental impairment, and severe mental impairment would not be appropriate. BASW is less specific wanting CTOs to apply to all forms of mental disorder.

There is, however, general agreement that the long-term schizophrenic patients would be the most appropriate group. These, according to the Royal College have had a history of compulsory in-patient treatment. But how many such patients would be likely to be put on a CTO? The Royal College do not say. However, using figures derived from a response to the Mental Health Act Commission discussion paper, E Bromley says of one Health Region in England and Wales that there were at least four patients likely to qualify and in one district he thought there were about six (Bromley, 1987, mimeo). The CTO would be a very large statutory instrument to deal with a very small problem.

If the long-term schizophrenic group of patients were to be the target then the legal drafting would need to be tight. It would have to include these and exclude all others. We do not believe however this would be the main problem, difficult though that may be. We think there would soon be demands to change and widen the target group. We think a second group of patients would be identified and would also said to be able to benefit from a CTO. Then a third and so on. All would be said to have special needs and require special attention. Later the CTO would include all the mentally disordered and would be a self-generating control system.

Even if not, and even if the target group were small there would be a ripple effect throughout the entire system. If the CTO were only for compulsory in-patients we think it would lead to an increase in the use of compulsory orders – for that would be the only way to secure a CTO on discharge. (And if for compulsory schizophrenic patients only, then an increase in compulsory admission for that type of patient and, dare we suggest it, a corresponding shift in diagnosis to meet that criteria.) If the CTO were to be drafted wider still to include all patients, compulsory or otherwise, there could be an increase in admissions to meet the criteria for a CTO. But even if not we would still have the alarming spectacle of a person seeking treatment on a voluntary basis entering hospital yet capable of being subject to a CTO on discharge.

And if the CTO were to be drafted so wide as to meet the Royal College's suggestion that 'the main criteria . . . would be that the patient requires compulsory treatment and that the treatment can be satisfactorily provided in the community rather than in hospital . . . ', what then? The Royal College say 'an important criterion would be that the patient should have had a previous period of severe mental illnesses which responded to medication. Previous in-patient detention would not be a requirement'. But what does that mean? Is it, as Lucy Scott-Moncrieff suggests, deliberately ambiguous (Scott-Moncrieff, 1988), or is there a suggestion that the CTO should include out-patients? And would these have had treatment from general practitioners, or the community psychiatric team? Suddenly we find the target group of patients increases with every proposal and with each new statement. The spectre of a control system not dissimilar from that for offenders looms large and becomes an increasing possibility. And why not include the 'worried well' or any other group perceived as a problem?

Aside from matters of definition, what would be the social and medical characteristics of the patient? Again it depends on the tightness of the criteria. If the patients selected are to be the long-term schizophrenic then typically they are male, young (under 35), unemployed, from social classes 4 and 5, and living in or around the inner city areas. They tend to live in hostels or other forms of subtenured accommodation – though if they were itinerants there would be no point in placing them on an order. If the nets were cast wider still to include all the mentally disordered, even the 'worried well', then a group more representative of the population generally would be included.

Consider for a moment this group of so-called long-term schizophrenic patients. Bromley describes them as a group of patients who would have been treated, probably compulsorily with neuroleptic medication over a considerable period of time. They would have responded to medication with a certain professionally judged good effect, yet are still so deluded that they resist the continuation of that same medication, or so deviant that they prefer being ill to being well. They would have not complied with professional advice or persuasion and may require threats to induce compliance. They would have enough insight to understand something of what is going on but not enough to function without sanctions (Bromley, 1987). The disposition of such patients would be awkward, difficult and contentious, even with medication. Bromley's point is that there are not many patients able to meet that criteria and he too fears that these new legal powers would be extended to include wider groups. We think it could soon include a population of people confined to prison who would then be put on CTO's on 'discharge' or released from prison, as a condition of parole.

It is clear that the tighter the criteria the more the patients selected will resemble the inadequate type of offenders familiar to the Courts, probation and penal system. Those offenders have social profiles similar to that of long-term schizophrenics – and may even be one and the same group. They rarely live with their immediate families, are often unemployed, are semi-itinerant, awkward and difficult to deal with and fail to learn from experience. Their success rates on probation are low, and the quality of supervision is of necessity restricted. Socially and economically they have few skills, and their class position makes it unlikely that they would have access to the social and institutional supports which would enable them to improve. Their social isolation is their downfall. If this is the sort of person suggested by the Royal College as candidates for the CTO it is unlikely that they will be a success and less likely they will cooperate on the order.

To be placed on a CTO, the Royal College says, the patient would need to be sufficiently ill to require compulsory admission yet presumably not quite ill enough to prevent treatment being provided in the community. The application of a CTO would be made on the grounds that 'it is necessary for the health and safety of the patient and for the protection of other persons that he should receive such treatment and it cannot be provided . . . unless he receives such treatment under the Section . . . ' I ·yal College of Psychiatrists, 1978, para. 3.1). No evidence seems ∞ be required of prior out-patient deterioration nor of 'the health or safety of the patient or the protection of other persons . . . '. Given the increasing criticisms of clinicians' ability to predict danger-ousness one would have thought it reasonable to have minimised fears about the indiscriminate use of such orders. Nor is it clear if the levels of dangerousness – whether to self or others – would be different for those required for a CTO than for patients being compulsorily admitted. We think *prima facie* that there should be: the compulsory admission procedure is designed to take patients out of one setting and put them in a more restrictive one, whereas a CTO involves leaving the patient in a setting with few immedi-ate controls except those provided by the patient's medication. Clearly if the patient poses a danger to himself or others he should be hospitalised under Section 3, and should only be allowed to return to the community when the threat is diminished. We are not told if this is to be so. Should there be a greater threat for an in-patient than for someone on a CTO? If so, how much greater? Again no answers are given – at least for the proposals from the Royal College or BASW.

Making and applying the order

The second question concerns how it would operate. Here there are clear differences between BASW's proposals – where the so-cial worker would make and supervise the order, and the Royal College who somewhat naturally say they would want to do it. If BASW's views are accepted, it is difficult to see how these propos-als differ in substance from the existing Guardianship orders – for guardianship too was intended to be local-authority-based and local-authority-managed.

The Royal College suggests that a CTO should be made after an application from the nearest relative or an Approved Social Worker. The wording of the application would follow that of Section 3(2)(a) of the 1983 Act except that 'in a hospital' would be replaced by 'in the community' and subsequent references to 'detention' omitted. However, in line with the Royal College's contention (even if it is not altogether clear what the intention is), that the CTO should be for in-patients only, it proposes that a new subsection should be inserted to say 'that the patient has had a previous period of severe mental illness which responded to medication'.

BASW has an altogether different view. BASW proposes two types of order: first, an interim Community Care Order lasting 72 hours operating along the lines of the emergency order (section 4); second, as full CTO would be like the compulsory order of Section 3. BASW says, 'The social worker would have responsibility relating not only to whether or not a Community Care Order is appropriate, but also to how it is carried out (BASW, 1977, para. 4.2(b)). Both orders would be backed by the Local Authority, the social worker having the power to direct the authority initially to act as a care expert for a period of 72 hours. Thereafter the local authority would have power to confirm the extension and duration of the order.

These orders would run alongside existing provisions, whether under Section 117 of the 1983 Act – which imposes on the Mental Health Authority and Local Authority a duty to provide joint after-care – or as Guardianship Orders. There is no suggestion that existing orders be removed, modified or given up. The CTO would therefore extend compulsory powers, adding to and increasing the kinds of patients on supervision and adding to the powers of the supervisors. It would not, however, produce a new group of supervisors: social workers and psychiatrists already have considerable powers under the 1983 Mental Health Act, though it might enlarge the numbers of people involved in supervision. We think however that psychiatrists would delegate their power to others in the community team, leaving them to make day-to-day supervisory contacts – unless such delegation was prohibited. But whatever method is chosen it is likely the community team would relay appropriate information back to the psychiatrist. In this way the psychiatrists would become second-order supervisors. In contrast the community team would have less or no direct power, although of course it would retain a great deal of influence and input into the supervisory process. It is interesting that the Royal College made no mention of supervision, and by avoiding it passed over some of the critical questions. BASW at least confronted the problem: the social worker would carry out the supervision through the powers delegated by the local social services department.

The Royal College gives details of the extent of the order (to last 6 months), but tells us nothing of the nature of that supervision. Would the supervisor take the patient to an out-patient clinic if the patient refused to go? Would the police stand over the patient whilst s/he washed and dressed? And would the police break down the patients' door every morning to allow a community psychiatric nurse to see how the patient was getting on? (Scott-Moncrieff, 1988). Are we therefore to accept Lucy Scott-Moncrieff's conclusion that in spite of the Royal College's claim to the contrary we should stop talking of compulsory nursing in the community, compulsory care in the community or compulsory habilitation and rehabilitation (Scott-Moncrieff, 1988). For to do so raises expectations that cannot be fulfilled. But if not the police, who else? Would the psychiatric team be granted powers of arrest or detention similar to those of the police? If so this would clearly expose the supervisor to the accusation that control was emphasised at the expense of treatment, and coercion at the expense of freedom. The Royal College's use of the word 'treatment' is thus misleading. It helps to slide over the nature of the task.

The Royal College also fails to come to grips with the questions of control. It sees the CTO and the types of patient to be replaced on a CTO as belonging to a group who could be threatened and cajoled into agreement. It does not seem to occur to the Royal College that the CTO would be for dissenting patients or for those unable to cope, or for those wanting to cope but without the wherewithal to do so. It also assumes that once compliance is obtained treatment will proceed in an orderly manner. Again, this is disingenuous. The Royal College above all else must know the disposition of mental patients and know too that compliance will be rare for the type of patient they suggest to be on a CTO.

Yet even if compliance could be achieved readily and easily there would still be limitations on the nature of the treatments to be provided. Nursing care or rehabilitation would be difficult to give to these patients – for the reasons cited earlier. There would be few possibilities to provide therapies. The most likely types of treatment to be given would be ECT or depot neuroleptics. That in itself raises tricky questions: would this perhaps encourage greater use of such treatments? And if so what would be the long-term effects? It has been estimated that neuroleptics are effective for about 25 per cent of the patients for another 25 per cent are ineffective and for the other 50 per cent extremely varied (MIND, 1987). The Mental Health Act Commission is correct therefore in drawing attention to a profound ethical dilemma about forcing patients to take medication which may have unpleasant and dis-abling side-effects and which may possibly not be of benefit to them (MHAC, 1986).

Leading on from this then is the equally important question is how does a patient get off the order? How is the patient to be discharged? The Royal College talks of an order lasting 6 months with opportunities for renewal – the patients presumably remain-ing on medication for most of the time. The Royal College adds that there should be a right of appeal to a Mental Health Review Tribunal (MHRT) provided as a matter of urgency within a few days of being placed on the order. This is misleading. It is not always possible to get a MHRT in a few days. Nor without changes in the duties of the MHRTs would it be the appropriate body to have them deal with CTOs. MHRTs are required to say whether or not a patient requires hospitalisation – they are not able to say whether or not a patient can function in the community without medication.

Assume that the patient takes medication regularly and is sta-bilised on neuroleptic drugs, and agrees to continue taking med-ication. That would seem to be grounds for discharging the order; or at least not renewing it after 6 months. Or would something more be required; an improvement in the psychiatric condition or active demonstration of one's sanity? But how does one demon-strate one's sanity? Will there be drug-free periods with an oppor-tunity to show how one has regained sanity without medication? And how does a patient show that he has improved and will continue to improve? Or worse still, how does he show that he will not relapse? The odds become heavily stacked against pa-tients for they are required to show more than could reasonably be expected of them: more than the normal out-patient and more than others who have never been psychiatric patients. As with all such things, it is easier to show that professional help is required than to show it is not. It is also easier to justify retaining a patient on an order than to justify discharging him.

A similar confusion appears in the way the Royal College deals with matters of consent to treatment: and again it is interesting to note that the second version hardly mentions consent, perhaps because of the criticisms the first version attracted. In the first the Royal College says:

> The consent to treatment provisions under Part 4 of the Mental Health Act should apply, but the provisions for the registered medical practitioner appointed for the purpose to consult with a nurse and other person are not appropriate particularly as no nurse might be involved at this stage. The College would recommend that these provisions be extended so that those patients who refuse medication could have *immediate* [emphasis original] access to a second opinion approved doctor under Section 58 (rather than after three months as at present): for these purposes a treatment plan is required (Royal College of Psychiatrists, 1987).

On the face of it and in strictly legal terms there is nothing contentious here: these proposals would bring the consent provisions in line with those for compulsory admitted patients. However the matter is more complicated than this especially when applied to a community setting.

We can see it this way: many of the assumptions underlying the CTO are that it is possible to transfer controls from the hospital to the community as if the community was an extension of the hospital, or, if not, then no different in aims or objectives. Yet we want to insist that it is not simply a matter of transferring hospital-based procedures to a community, and nowhere is this better illustrated than for consent. In the hospital consent-procedures are about whether the patient has a right to refuse to take medication. A CTO on the other hand, is about powers to require patients to take that medication in setting in which the patient is reasonably competent to operate. Indeed MIND has argued that a patient who is well enough to look after himself outside hospital is entitled to decide whether to take the drugs offered (MIND, 1987). But this is not how the Royal College sees things. It sees patients in terms of their illness and sees any refusal to take medication as a further indication that they are ill. Consent procedures, in the view of the Royal College, are about agreeing to the correct treatment, not about choosing to take treatment. This point is central to the debate.

For example, under the 1983 Act no distinction is made between the patient who is judged unable to give consent and someone who is capable of doing so but chooses otherwise. Yet, as Bromley says, the types of patients likely to be on a CTO will actually have dissented from the professional view of what is good for them in terms of medication. They are the groups who have chosen not to take treatment, their choice may be wrong, ill-conceived or whatever, but they have made that choice nonetheless (Bromley, 1989). The muddle into which the Royal College get themselves is because they cannot accept this. They see refusal as a symptom of illness. Hence they justify a CTO on the basis that the patient will not take medication; they cannot see that refusal to take it may be rational and justified, – or that the patient has willingly chosen to go along that road.

What would the sanctions be?

The Royal College and BASW both agree that there would be sanctions: they say they should involve compulsory admission to a hospital, although BASW talks of 'alternative methods of treatment which might include admission to hospital and a more contained environment' (BASW, 1976, para. 4.2(i)). When and how should such sanctions be applied? The answer to the first is: 'when patients refuse to take their medication'. BASW talks of 'patients who refuse or are unable to fulfil the conditions implied by the making of a CCO', and the Royal College of a 'refusal to accept medication'. The Royal College also talks of 'a period of consideration and negotiation with the patient' and whilst it argues that sanctions should 'not be an immediate response', it does not advise 'waiting too long when the patient begins to deteriorate for that would be against the whole purpose of the Order'. BASW on the other hand puts his faith in a Code of Practice. How should the sanctions be applied? The Royal College does not say, nor does BASW: presumably the patient would be detained in a place of safety in the first instance or taken directly to a hospital.

There is something odd about a proposal from the Royal College of Psychiatrists which sees the mental hospital as a sanction. Over the years the rhetoric has been of the hospital as a therapeutic institution directed towards treating an illness; what would one think of the general hospital being a sanction for those patients who failed to take medication prescribed by their hospital doctor, or their GP? Sociologists have been accused of distorting the true face of psychiatry by insisting that the mental hospital is an institution of control, yet here we see the Royal College of Psychiatrists saying something similar. 'There needs to be a sanction in the case of refusal (to take treatment) and the appropriate sanction is thought to be admission to hospital' (Royal College of Psychiatrists, April 1987, para. 4).

Compulsory admission to the mental hospital is only one possibility: another is to have sanctions but not use them. And a third is to impose treatment in the community with force if needs be. The Royal College favour the second, i.e. in having sanctions but not using them. They say it will be sufficient that the patient on a CTO realises that compulsion is available. It is difficult to take this argument seriously. Why should anyone take their medication and put up with unpleasant side-effects, when there are no sanctions to enforce it? And who would administer the treatment if the patient refused? The community psychiatric nurses have said that they would not be prepared to administer it because they think it would not be appropriate. One can see why. Consider the unedifying spectacle of police, nursing staff and family holding down a patient in his own home or on the street whilst he was given medication. So that leaves the other possibility: compulsory readmission to the mental hospital as the only available choice – that is, of course, if there are places available given the run-down of the hospital system.

Here we come to the nub of the debate. When should the sanctions be applied, and what are the purposes of the sanctions? It seems that sanctions are likely to be applied at one or two stages – Bromley calls them *trigger-points* (Bromley, 1987). The first would be when the patient refuses to comply with treatment but could still function adequately, the second when his condition had deteriorated. These two points are not identical: refusal to accept treatment may not accompany deterioration thought it might. Leaving aside the question whether it does or not, a rather odd situation could develop where patients are compulsory admitted, not because they are ill but because they do not take their medication and the psychiatrist predicts future illness. Bromley puts it this way: 'We could have the spectacle of an adequately functioning person, possibly one who is psychiatrically symptom-free compulsorily admitted and detained in hospital' (Bromley, 1978). The paradox is evident. We would then have legislation which allows an adequately functioning individual to be compulsorily admitted to hospital in order to impose a community treatment order which was introduced to prevent readmission to hospital in the first place (ibid). Clearly the first trigger-point produces a curious result. Might it then be better to wait for the second trigger-point when the patient's condition has deteriorated before doing something?

But the second trigger-point produces an equally curious situation. Assume that the patient's condition had deteriorated to the point where he needed compulsory admission. In this case why should the patient need a CTO? As there are adequate existing facilities under current legislation a second order would merely duplicate procedures – unless, that is, a CTO would allow the patient to be admitted under less stringent evidence than before, i.e. would need to be less ill or show less deterioration than was necessary for Section 3. The Royal College seem to be aware of this but not apparently of its implications. They say 'To wait until the patient has deteriorated to a serious degree however would be against the whole purpose of the Order' (Royal College of Psychiatrists, para 6, October 1987). Presumably this means before the patient meets the requirements of Section 3. This is rather an odd position to be in. It will mean there will be a two-track system of compulsory admission, one using less stringent criteria than the other.

Part of the confusions exist because the Royal College uses such terms as deterioration and non-compliance as if they were interchangeable. It talks initially of non-compliance or refusal. ('There needs to be a procedure to follow in the case of refusal', or 'It is anticipated that having been placed on a CTO, most patients will then agree to treatment' (Royal College of Psychiatrists, para. 6, October 1987)). Later the Royal College talks of deterioration and clearly links the two. 'To wait until the patient has deteriorated to a serious degree, however, would be against the whole purpose of the order.' To see the extent of the confusion assume that there are two patients on a CTO. Patient *A* refuses to take medication and remains relatively stable (non-compliant), whilst Patient *B* takes his but gets worse (deterioration). Neither wishes to return to hospital. Who should then be compulsorily readmitted? Presumably both: Patient *A* because of his non-compliance, and Patient *B* because of his deterioration. But why? In our view such a system will only lead to confusion and will be seen as unjustified and unfair.

Another part of the confusion arises because the CTO is trying to do two things:

1. recreate the hospital control system in the community;
2. operate on the basis that the community is a less-restrictive hospital.

But the 'community' – whatever that may mean – is not a therapeutic milieu. The community produces different sets of social rules, including giving different freedoms to patients. Out-patient treatment is not, nor ever can be the same as, treatment in hospital under a more related setting.

Rights and liberties

Robert Miller argues that the move towards a CTO in the USA, has received much impetus from the repressive conditions of many mental hospitals. In Britain the Royal College might not see it in such stark terms. It bases its own position on the spirit of the 1983 Act: that is, to provide treatment in the least restrictive alternative. It also notes changes in psychiatric practice: increasingly patients are managed outside hospital and admission rates are low. Miller notes that civil libertarians in the USA have generally favoured the CTO (called out-patient commitment) as an alternative to hospitalisation. Their version of success is measured by the numbers prevented from entering hospitals rather than the efficacy of the treatments provided. He adds that despite giving general support to a CTO, American libertarians have still been critical of the practice, focusing most of their criticisms on the lack of community resources. Without resources CTOs become mere preventive detention (Miller, 1988a).

Civil libertarians in Britain tend to see the CTO rather differently. They see it as a controlling mechanism, potentially increasing psychiatric power and producing additional restraints. It is not that the CTO would reduce admissions, for admissions have been dramatically reduced in the last decade anyway. Nor is it that the CTO would speed up transfers from hospital, for they have been speeded up likewise. It is that the CTO will increase the numbers placed on orders and so increases the controls. Patients discharged from hospital will be controlled when they would have been merely out-patients. Out-patients who have not been to hospital, nor are likely to go there, could be placed on CTOs. Such controls are seen as wrong in principle and flawed in the justifications used to support them.

Some civil libertarians look beyond proposals for the CTO and emphasise further the potential to restrict freedoms. Already they say there are talk of 'tagging' patients on a CTO. (What on earth are to be the sanctions for those breaking the 'tag' – commitment to hospital perhaps?). And what will come after that? There has always been a fear amongst British civil libertarians that controls are imposed first and manipulation follows. The 'less restrictive' nature of the CTO might prove illusory because of the increased potential to monitor and control patients' lives. Some of the more militant ex-patients in the USA would agree. Miller points to certain former patients who argue that autonomy is more important than treatment no matter how well-intentioned and beneficial that treatment might be. Even adequate resources do not justify imposing out-patient treatment. (Miller, 1988a).

It may be possible to hedge the CTO with restrictions to meet some of these criticisms. For example, patients might not be placed on a CTO unless it was demonstrated that without treatment they would be dangerous: there would need to be evidence of prior out-patient deterioration or of dangerous behaviour which required hospitalisation. Or perhaps prior evidence of recent deterioration. If so, clinicians might be expected to oppose such restrictions – preferring the more open-ended terminology currently used in the 1983 Act (i.e. 'it is necessary for the health or safety of the patient or for the protection of other persons that he should receive such treatment'). Clinicians might also argue against leaving patients until their behaviour deteriorated. They might want to intervene earlier. But how dangerous is that dangerous behaviour to be, and what does dangerous mean in this context? What would be the evidence and the source of that evidence?

Before embarking on a programme for CTOs we ought to look carefully at other fields to see what can be learned there. Whilst it may be true that we should be careful about importing results from one country to another there are parallels in the criminal justice field. Strangely enough those proposing the CTOs have studiously avoided looking at this. Had they done so they would notice how other mechanisms such as probation, parole, intermediate treatment (for juveniles) etc., designed to provide less restrictive alternatives to custody have rarely fulfilled their rehabilitation promises (Bean, 1976; Miller, 1988b). Rather, they have produced new control networks more extensive than before, with little to suggest that the offenders have benefited. It is not possible here to go over the vast literature which shows that the rehabilitative ideal produces few benefits for the offender whilst providing considerably more for those operating the system, but those data cannot be ignored.

At one level the mental-health and penal systems are different: mental health supervision will not be the same as for offenders on a probation order. Mental-health systems do not rely on the courts to define the orders – except in the USA of course. But there are similarities, whether of ideology or of structure, and a similarity in the views, whether in attitudes or life styles of those at the receiving end. Warnings from the criminal justice system ought not go unheeded. The demise in the rehabilitative ideal has been followed by increasing Government pressure to increase the levels of supervision in the community, with pressure on the probation service to act as surveillance officers offering a cheaper alternative to prison. Those supporting the CTO would be well-advised to note this trend lest they too end up as surveillance officers – albeit in the mental-health service.

Conclusion

Proposals for the CTO reflect the changing nature of psychiatric practice. The demise in the influence of the mental hospital and the corresponding use in importance of the community, have been largely responsible: in a world where fewer patients are admitted, and almost all are discharged, and then rather quickly, proposals for the CTO have found fertile soil in which to take root and flourish. Sometimes they have been offered as a way of assisting discharge, speeding it up or reducing readmission – in which case they have been relevant to the main theme of this book. Sometimes, too, they have been offered as a form of out-patient supervision, almost as a supervision/probation order, in which case they have been less directly relevant. It has, however, been difficult to separate them, and for convenience they have been included together as one package.

Whether CTOs are to be used for discharges or not we have tried to show that the purposes behind the CTO fall short in many respects. Often there is a lack of clarity about the reasons for a CTO, and some proposals seem unduly optimistic about the outcome. Others fail because they do not consider the experiences gained in the penal system which the CTO closely resembles. Moreover, as we keep saying, we do not think that it is sufficient to see a shift in treatment from the hospital to the community and we do not believe that hospital control systems can be transported to the community. The settings are different. To ignore those differences distorts the position of the patients and the nature of the supervision. It also makes mockery of any talk of sanctions.

6

The Rights of People with Mental Health Problems in the Community

Changes in psychiatric practices, and in the position of the mental hospital, do not of course take place in a vacuum. They affect everyone and every part of the system. When patients are no longer treated in mental hospitals – or rather spend less time there than before – and are treated in the community, wholesale changes and adjustments have to be made. One such adjustment concerns patients' rights, whether of their rights whilst receiving community treatment, or their right to be free of that treatment. This is not an area which is well-documented – indeed the question of patients' rights generally or even of rights in hospital has been left largely unexplored. Yet we think this is an important area and one which will assume increasing importance as community care develops, irrespective of the form that care may take. Societies which opt for a community-care approach promote new questions about patients' rights. And as we will show throughout this chapter they are questions which have few answers as yet.

In this chapter we wish to look at the nature of those patients' rights, as they exist now and as they are determined by law. Under common law 'legal systems' means both tort and statute law. We now wish to see if rights exist for patients within the community and finally look at some of the criticisms of what are called 'right-based strategies'. These questions are easily related to empirical matters nor can generalisation be made outside specific legal systems. Rights are very much produced by and part of a national culture: rights in Britain differ from rights in Canada, or the USA let alone in continental Europe. What we wish to do here is to make some specific points and hope that in so doing we move the subject on a little so that wider generalisation can be made later.

Patients rights generally

The demands that mental patients be accorded certain rights has been a clarion call of civil libertarians for decades. The civil libertarian task is a difficult one and the struggle likely to remain protracted. All too often mental patients have lost basic rights when they have entered the care of mental-health specialists. In England and Wales, this was particularly so under the 1959 Mental Health Act in which a belated attempt was made to restore some of these rights under the 1983 Mental Health Act, but this too was limited. Consent to treatment, for example, which is a basic right given to all other medical patients was introduced but the provisions were half-hearted: they have not given the patient the right to refuse treatment but instead have provided the patient with a second medical opinion – an altogether different matter (see Bean, 1986) – albeit an independent medical opinion appointed and approved by a body designed to protect patients' right, e.g. the Mental Health Act Commission (MHAC), but only a second opinion nonetheless.

One can see why civil libertarians labour under such disadvantages. Patients with mental health problems are not a group whose cause is easy to espouse. They are not given the sympathy often granted to victims of crime, for too often they are the perpetrators of discord: frequently they are perceived as dangerous whether to the social order, to others or to themselves. When they are also offenders they are regarded with additional apprehension for their unpredictable behaviour rightly arouses fears. Almost, by definition the mad are estranged from social relationships, living in their isolated worlds, and difficult to reach in the emotional sense. Not being responsible for their actions they can easily be regarded as forfeiting basic rights unless or until they return to an accepted level of responsibility. Lacking responsibility they are also seen as lacking other qualities which demand citizenship. As a social group they command little political power, and rarely need to be taken seriously – by this we mean that their demands can be regarded as the outcome of their mental condition and their claims easily sidestepped. They lack the appeal and the power to operate as a successful pressure group. All too often others must act in their stead.

It is not so much that users of psychiatric services are stripped of their rights, although some are. Sometimes the rights given to them are inappropriate or the wrong sort. The so-called 'right to treatment' under earlier legislation is an example which was dominated by a view that key decisions should be made by the medical profession. It turned out to be a mixed blessing. On the one hand it provided treatment to those who needed it and who may have welcomed psychiatric intervention, yet on the other it granted excessive powers to the psychiatrist – often accompanied by a patronising view which offered little in the way of legal protection. Moreover that right to treatment often excluded other rights: for example, the right to privacy. Privacy allows the patients to retain a degree of social space but this of course could be seen as intruding on the therapeutic relationship and interfering with treatment. It produced conflict and became an obstacle to the medical approach. As such it was unacceptable.

Rarely has the so-called right to treatment existed in it pure form, nor has it been enshrined in statutes – except by implication. More likely psychiatrists merely acted as if it was. Yet typically when patients have a right to treatment they are rarely asked their opinions or given choices about their treatment. Their rights, such as they are, are couched in medical terms. The advantage to the patient is that it grants the physician a duty and an obligation to provide treatment when the patient requires it. Yet the disadvantages are unclear. Armed with such a world view and supported by an ideology which refers to treatment as always being in the patient's best interests, and buttressed by a view that psychiatry offers a humanitarian service, it becomes possible to do almost anything to the patient. And so it has been. If that involved the removal of brain tissue, the continued use of heavy tranquillisers, or numerous doses of ECT, so be it. The history of psychiatry since 1945 in most Western societies has been one of the patient receiving what was given to him even if that treatment was of a most extreme form.

Fortunately we no longer accept that simple view of medical dominance. Nor do we now believe that psychiatry should produce dependent patients. We are beginning to accept that patients can make decisions for themselves, and are able to know their best interests even if they are mentally disordered. Above all we now believe that patients are able to question the views of the professionals, and if rights such as the right to privacy threaten the stability of the doctor–patient relationship then the professionals must concede. The mood is changing. In contrast to the situation a decade ago, professionals must justify their actions and the patients are beginning to see that they can have a stake in their treatment programme.

But to talk of such changes is only part of the picture, for the patients' rights debate implies that patients are the only group having or needing rights. We think the area is much wider than this. We believe that rights should be ascribed to all who work in the mental-health field, not just to patients. Hitherto rights have been narrowly defined: the talk was only of 'patients' rights' – rarely there has been consideration of the rights of those conducting treatment. One can of course see why. Rights, traditionally, have been about control: patients are the least powerful, those conducting treatment are more so. But we think this view of rights misses some of the complexities of treatment, not the least the role of the State, or of other agencies so involved. We want to see those who have direct contact with the patients as not being all-powerful; they, too, are at their receiving end and have others in power over them, whether as employers, the State or both. But even this is too simple: among the treating group there are various subgroups with different status divisions each of which has a different level of power: physicians are more powerful than nurses who are more powerful than social workers, and so on. Rights for all these groups need to be considered. We wish to argue that the term 'patients' rights' in the modern world has been too exclusive, and we wish to enlarge it to include all involved in treatment: patients, physicians and advocates alike.

Positive rights and claim rights

Discussions about rights have a long philosophical heritage. Philosophers have classified rights in various ways: economic, legal, social, moral, etc., according to the type of activity or interest that the right protects. Or rights have been classified according to the way they are established or maintained (Benn, and Peters, 1975, p. 93). Thus, for these purposes we might distinguish between legal rights and moral rights, the former established and upheld by state institutions, the latter upheld by opinion. Legal rights we can call positivist – i.e. a right may be said to exist when there is reasonable ground for the expectation that it will be upheld by law. A positivist right, or a positivist theory of rights says there is no right where there is no power to secure the object of the right. By this we mean that the power arises from the exercise of a coercive sanction to enforce that correlative duty (Benn and Peters, 1975, p. 91). When we look at moral rights we find that they differ – the crucial difference being they have not been established by law. That is, unless based on law they are simply demands or claims from those who believe that such rights ought to exist and ought to be legally enforced. In a sense they are more about future policy and the direction of change. For example, we may claim that people suffering mental distress have a moral right to asylum. But unless or until the law says this is so the claim is not substantiated. It is directed towards producing a new policy or subverting an old one which we may dislike perhaps because it has (say) reduced mental-hospital places or some other reason. Or we may say there is a moral right for advocates to represent patients in the courts, or negotiate for patients with hospital managers about conditions. But again unless or until the law says so these claims are similar to that above. They are *claim* rights: they are about what ought to be.

The point about this brief excursion into rights theory is to show that debates about patients' rights, have to be tied to wider questions about rights generally. For these purposes when we talk of rights we shall mean *positive* rights, which in this case mean those provided by tort and statute law. We wish to confine the discussion to positive rights, the aim being to find out what rights exist rather than embark on the wider discussions of moral rights and claim rights and debate what ought to be. Yet when we look at positive rights, those derived from tort and statute law it appears that these laws have not caught up with changes in psychiatric practice. There is in Britain very little case law on the rights of people in mental hospitals and very little elsewhere. In contrast there is considerably more available about claim rights i.e. there is a large debate about what ought to be, and especially about what ought to be concerning the appropriate levels of resources or care to secure those claims. That debate will no doubt continue and may influence rights in the future. But this is not what interests us here. To find what exists now, especially rights for patients in the community we must identify such rights and later consider some of the difficulties securing those rights through the courts. For as all positivists insist it is one thing to believe rights exist, still another to have them implemented. And arriving at that second stage can be no less daunting. It can also be an expensive and protracted business.

Rights in law

For patients seeking to know their legal rights, the task is far from easy. Margaret Brazier points out that the law relating to medical and psychiatric practice has to be discovered from a variety of sources. In Britain the regulation of medical practice and the disciplining of the defaulting doctor is entrusted by Act of Parliament to the General Medical Council under the Medical Act 1983. Other countries have different methods. Again in Britain the structure of the National Health Service is governed by several statutes which also embody rules dealing with complaints procedures under the NHS. The Medicines Acts are concerned with the safety of drugs. There are also Statutory Instruments which provide regulations about a variety of matters such as the duties of GPs etc. (Brazier, 1987). Other countries have similarly complex requirements. But these are by no means all. Much law remains judge-made derived from common law – which applies to the USA and most English-speaking countries. Decisions and judgements are handed down by the courts. These provide precedents for determining later disputes. They also define the rights and duties of doctors and patients in areas untouched by statute, e.g. the common law governs questions of compensation for medical accident as well as the rights of parents to control the medical treatment of their children (Brazier, 1987, p. 3).

In countries with a common-law tradition tort law is concerned with claims of negligence. For our purposes this means negligent treatment following contact between patients and physician – or more specifically the psychiatrist. The function of tort law is to compensate an individual injured by another's error, not to adjudicate on a physician's general competence (Jones, 1989). Actions against physicians, however, are perceived by the Medical Defence Societies as attacks on the physicians' professional integrity and a potential blight on the physicians' career. They are usually defended vigorously through the combative nature of the legal system. It is not appropriate here to go into some of the obvious disadvantages of a tort system, nor of its unfairness except to ask what is the justification for giving one person who can attribute his injury to human error full compensation while another whose injury has some other cause receives no compensation at all. A no-fault scheme as recommended by the Pearson Commission and as operates, for example, in New Zealand offers distinct advantages (HMSO, 1978, Pearson Commission; Brazier, 1987, p. 144).

Tort law offers the possibility of claims for negligence against groups possessing certain skills – which for our purposes means psychiatrists though it could equally be other members of the medical and allied professions. (We are not here concerned with rights outside the doctor/patient relationship). Patients' rights under the laws of tort consist of enforcing claims against those with a duty to care – the most obvious type of claim would be against negligent treatment. Tort law is concerned with the intentional violation of the private rights of others, and the negligent abrogation of legally recognised duties of care to others (Posser, 1971).

Whereas tort law concerns matters of professional negligence statute law grants the patients more specific rights, such as those under the compulsory admission procedures. However, in England and Wales statute law has rarely produced rights that are completely unequivocal or which spell out the patient's position or lists restrictions to be imposed on others. Rather, it has offered rights of a more negative nature: for example, the right to be compulsorily treated only in accordance with procedures determined by Act of Parliament; or the right not to be compelled to accept medication except where the law says so, or the right not to be forcibly removed from home except by procedures granted in law (i.e. Section 135 of the 1983 Mental Health Act). In the USA rights are more clearly stated and the rights of patients determined clearly, often of course linked to the Constitution.

Patients' rights under statute law have recently been the subject of some scrutiny, especially those rights related to compulsory admissions to mental hospitals and those concerned with consent to treatment or with treatment generally. This trend has occurred throughout the Western world although there are still some countries in Europe, where this is not so. Mental hospitals in Greece, for example, detain patients in appalling conditions whilst Norway seems content with over 80 per cent of patients having compulsory orders placed upon them. The number of deaths recorded in Japanese mental hospitals remains unacceptably high. There is of course value in prioritising a debate about these matters and we hope that the debate will continue, although what is needed is something stronger than a debate: what is needed is an organisation with the international prestige of Amnesty International able to identify and publicise areas where rights are being trampled on. But that is a long way in the future.

Securing rights

Whatever the rights of mental patients, even if defineable, they still need to be secured in court. Unhappily the law makes it difficult for patients to seek legal redress. It places many obstacles

in the way, with variations in the degree to which they are insurmountable. Consider some of the less difficult ones. Klein and
Glover make the point that although psychiatrists like other medical specialists can be sued for malpractice the number of claims
against them is still much fewer than in other medical fields. They
attribute this to the way psychiatry is practised compared with
other medical specialisations. Physicians are primarily concerned
with the treatment of physical illness, so that when they are
negligent the patient's illness is aggravated in some way, or a new
physical injury results. Psychiatrists deal with different problems:
generally they treat mental, emotional or behavioural disorders.
Negligence in psychiatry, say Klein and Glover, is no less real but
it does not cause physical injury, though it may aggravate pre-
existing emotional disorder (Klein and Glover, 1983). And being
emotional it is more difficult to identify.

Is psychiatry's favoured position changing? Again according
to Klein and Glover, the American experience would suggest that
it is. Recently there has been an increase in malpractice suites in
the USA challenging the use of ECT as well as consent procedures. Moreover, families of patients are increasingly pursuing
suits against psychiatrists for negligence. The most common one
occurs when the patient has committed suicide. Here negligence
would be alleged on the basis that the psychiatrist ought not to
have discharged the patient. Or negligence could be alleged where
the patient is convicted of homicide and it is again suggested that
the patient ought not to have been set free to be able to commit the
offence (Klein and Glover, 1983, p. 15).

The trend towards negligence is increasing in other countries
also. There is more litigation generally, and more against psychiatrists. In Britain the Medical Defence Union reports new and
increasing demands made upon it: an indication of the anxiety
which psychiatrists have about the possibilities of litigation being
promoted against them. The Medical Defence Union's advice and
opinions are now sought on such matters as the side-effects of
medication or on the implications for the psychiatrist if (say) the
psychiatrist has diagnosed a functional psychosis when there was
an underlying organic condition, or on consent to treatment; or on
matters relating to transfers from hospital as it seems that new
questions are being asked about the responsibilities of psychiatrists where patients are treated in the community. Apparently,
almost all the questions have one or two underlying themes. They
usually concern patients released from hospital who have injured

a third party there. Typically that third party would want to sue the patient and the patient would then want to sue the psychiatrist. Another theme is that a discharge patient attempts suicide, or that a discharge patient's condition deteriorates because s/he is receiving poor-quality care.

Yet in spite of increasing demands for advice the type of negligence case most likely to succeed at least in England and Wales is the so-called 'open window' case: literally one in which a psychiatrist has left a window open in the clinic or hospital and the patient has committed suicide by jumping out of the window, but metaphorically where any negligence has contributed to the death or injury of the patient. Successful actions which depend on the negligent administration of medication, or on emotional injury caused to the patient offer less hope of redress.

There are, it seems, many reasons why such negligence claims are difficult to bring to court, and more difficult to resolve once in the court. Tort law in Britain has been slow to provide remedies for purely emotional injuries – perhaps because emotional injuries *per se* are not recognised as injuries, or if they are, they are seen as much too difficult to identify and quantify. Some commentators suggest that the stigma of mental illness may dissuade some patients from filing a lawsuit. Or perhaps patients develop strong emotional ties to their psychiatrists which may make it difficult to institute legal proceedings. Klein and Glover say psychiatrists are trained to deal with their patients' hostility and this helps them to forestall a threatened lawsuit (see Klein and Glover, 1983). Yet even if patients are able to pursue their case to court would the courts favour them? Would, for example, emotional damage be accepted as a form of damage like physical damage? Some lawyers believe that it should, and say that mental distress is no less real and no more difficult to measure than physical pain, for which courts readily allow compensation. They say too that the difficulties of proving causation are overstated: mental disorders can often be traced directly to the defendant's action (see Klein and Glover, 1983, p. 132). Others disagree and see emotional damage as too nebulous, and too difficult to identify let alone quantify.

Then there are other obstacles that are more deliberate. In England and Wales the most obvious concerns Section 139. This section provides one of the most carefully orchestrated attempts to frustrate and prevent litigation under statute law. It is an obstacle of a peculiarly British, or rather English, Welsh or Southern

Irish nature, i.e. not Scottish or Northern Irish. It is rarely found outside the British Isles.

Briefly Section 139 of the Mental Health Act 1983 prevents mental patients from bringing a civil or criminal action against any person in any court in respect of an act done without the leave of the High Court or the Director of Prosecution. The justification for this type of legislation was given by Lord Simon in a judgement in the House of Lords, when he said that patients treated under mental health legislation, 'may generally be inherently likely to harass those concerned with them by groundless charges and litigations and may therefore have to suffer modification of this general right of access to the courts' (see Bean, 1986). (This section, which was then Section 141 of the 1959 Act but now 139 of the 1983 Act says 'no civil or criminal proceedings can be brought against any person in any court in respect of act done under the 1983 Act without the leave of the High Court or the Director of Public Prosecutions and for such proceedings to succeed the court must be satisfied that the person proceeded against acted in bad faith or without reasonable care.' The 1983 Act is a slight modification of that early legislation.) Lord Simon gave no evidence to support his views, nor does there seem to be any. Yet this comment explicitly gives support to legislation which is clearly discriminatory providing extraordinary protection for those conducting treatment.

If these obstacles are not enough patients usually face the additional one of having decisions made about them in secret and away from the public gaze. For example, patients admitted to hospital on a compulsory order usually have the order made in their own home or in the privacy of the hospital. In research on the way in which compulsory powers were operated it was found that more often than not patients were not told that they have been placed on a compulsory order let alone under which of the appropriate sections of the Mental Health Act they had been admitted (Bean, 1980). Things have improved in the last decade or so: patients at least have the right to have the order explained to them. But even so this catalogue of obstacles shows just how difficult and daunting it must be for patients to secure their rights when they believe that their rights have been violated.

All such obstacles are unwittingly helped by the nature and practice of psychiatry itself. By this we mean that psychiatry through no fault of its own places its own set of obstacles in front of the patient. We can see this more clearly if we compare psychi-

atry with other forms of medicine. First and foremost psychiatry
has no central orthodoxy. That is, there are no agreed standards of
care or procedures for undertaking treatment. A central orthodoxy implies an approved and accepted way of treating patients
according to certain conditions. (Treatment in this instance relates
inter alia to medication, levels of that medication and length of
treatment.) It also implies an acceptable way of nursing or managing the patient, with standardised sets and procedures to be used
when treatments fail. Psychiatry has none of these whereas all
exist with somatic medicine. Again psychiatrists keep no record
of any internal enquiry aimed at evaluating procedures. Yet without records obtaining evidence is almost impossible (see Bean,
1986).

We suggest too that lawyers have not seen mental health law
and patients' rights under tort law as a fruitful area of litigation.
Mental patients rarely make good witnesses, their allegations are
difficult to check and they are not the easiest of clients with whom
to deal. There are few financial rewards to recompense lawyers.
Moreover, to be successful lawyers must take on and win against
the full force of the medical profession. To succeed they need to
be acquainted with psychiatry – this means having a working
knowledge of psychiatric treatments and its effects. Understand-
ably most lawyers find more remunerative pickings elsewhere
involving less unpleasantness and frustration. Add to this, mental
health law is not a legal specialism favoured or taught in many
law departments of universities or polytechnics, with a few
notable exceptions, and this must increase the general level of
disadvantage.

Finally, another type of obstacle also less overt, but equally
difficult to overcome, is found in certain forms of statutory law
where the law lays duties on certain organisations such as local
authorities to provide services for mental patients but does nothing if the local authority fails to comply. Strictly speaking these
provisions cannot be regarded as giving positive rights to patients
for there is no possibility of forcing local authorities to provide
services. Rather the law *suggests* that local authorities should
provide them and it does nothing if the local authority chooses
otherwise. This has led Larry Gostin to propose what he calls an
'ideology of entitlement' meaning that access to health and social
services should not be based upon charitable or professional discretion but on enforceable rights (Gostin, 1983). Gostin says Par-

liament is not obliged to pass legislation to provide health and social services. But once it does it cannot arbitrarily deprive or exclude certain individuals or client groups. If there is an unreasonable denial of services the remedy should be provided by law. Often Parliament provides services such as after-care or day-care, or social-work services: it passes the legislation but the local authorities do nothing. What then? The mental patient cannot resort to law to insist on those services being provided. Larry Gostin wants to give the patient that right.

Gostin's 'ideology of entitlement', however, says nothing about the quality of the care to be provided. Nor could it. Rights are ill-suited to deal with matters of that complexity. For example, National Health Service employers or Local Authority Social Service Department could provide a basic service which fulfilled all statutory duties but did nothing else: they have granted the patient his rights, but that hardly amounts to much if the service is of little quality. An 'ideology of entitlement' would not cover that contingency. Larry Gostin is correct only in so far as he shows there is something amiss when Parliament passes legislation granting rights, and it is not implemented by those whose duty it is to do so, but he does not provide a blueprint which includes the quality of care.

The patient and community setting

The theme throughout this book is that the demise of the old-style mental hospital has been a major force for change. Almost all previous discussions of patients' rights have been set within what we call the institutional framework of psychiatry, i.e. the mental hospital, with little consideration given to treatment in the community. Again we can see why. Institutional psychiatry means hospital psychiatry and hospital practices have dictated the terms of reference. The Lunacy Act 1890, for example, was based on the fear that mental hospitals were secretive places and potential sources for abuse. Hence it provided detailed sets of rights for patients at various stages of their stay. There were rights about admission; rights about detention; rights about treatment and even rights about being absent without leave. (For example, if the patient was absent without leave for 28 days he could not be taken into custody, and ceased to be liable to detention. It was a right granted on the basis that a patient able to remain absent without leave for 28 days had proved that he could care for himself and did not require further detention. That right incidentally has remained under section 18(4) of the 1983 Act.)

Most of those rights were swept away by later legislation which centred on the right of the patient to receive treatment. Some were reinstated under the 1983 Act, very much akin to, and perhaps even influenced by, Gostin's 'new legalism', i.e. that patients should be placed under no extra jurisprudential social or political burdens on those designated unless they are justified by substantial and reasonable societal objectives. In practice this new legalism limits the exercise of psychiatric discretion by narrowing the criteria for admission, increasing control over the administration of certain treatments, and increasing the frequency of opportunity for legal review of the authorities to detain (Gostin, 1983). It does not, however, do much about the substance of patients' rights.

We do not wish to ignore the serious questions of patients' rights or the right of those conducting treatment within the mental hospital or create any impression that they are no longer important. Throughout the world there are still too many examples of patients being detained in appalling conditions and too many instances of patients not being accorded basic rights such as the right to refuse certain types of treatment or to be legally represented in an appeal, and too many instances of treatment staff being coerced into treating patients contrary to their professional ethics. But for these purposes we want to concentrate more on the implications of community treatment, for community treatment poses a new and untried set of problems which need attention.

Rights in the community

We can begin with a general proposition that rights for patients, whether in the community or not are based on the premise that patients can expect to receive a quality of care consistent with them as individuals – and presumably those undertaking treatment can expect to receive resources consistent with their task as treaters. That means that patients and treaters alike require protection from inhuman and degrading punishments, and need to be free of abuse, or arbitrary punishments and demeaning conduct. From studies of patients in the mental hospital we know that abuse is likely to be related to the length of stay, the size of the hospitals and the extent of seclusion surrounding the hospital.

Long-stay patients in large mental hospitals set apart from the community setting present the highest risk. As yet we know nothing about which patients present the highest risk in the community but we suspect it will be the frail, the elderly and those who have been and are chronically sick.

The second general point is a restatement of an earlier one: that is, the community is not an extension of the hospital, though it is sometimes seen as if it is. In an obvious sense the difference is about the amount of control to be exerted: out-patients and community treatments operate with more flexibility than in the hospital where doctor–patient contacts are less frequent. This means that any influences on the patient, other than by the treatment officials, are more difficult to determine, and the activities of the patients more difficult to control. In a hospital controls can be imposed and implemented. For example, psychiatrists can increase the levels of observation over the patient or order restraints where necessary, or spend extra time with the patient and encourage other staff and other patients to do likewise. In the last resort, the psychiatrist may prescribe medication or use therapeutic sanctions to control any immediate problem. These options are not available when the patient is treated in the community. The community psychiatrists' main option – and perhaps the only one when confronted with someone out of control – is to admit to hospital, perhaps on a compulsory order, and sedate immediately.

The community also differs from the hospital in that it lacks the goals to which hospitals aspire. Hospitals are therapeutic institutions directed towards dealing with mental disorders. The community is not: it may and often does have non-therapeutic intentions; though the more ardent supporters of community care have tended to overlook that. Indeed, there is little evidence to suggest that the community does care, nor will care in the future. At best some members of the community might care, but most are indifferent, and some are actively hostile.

What then are the specific rights of patients in the community? In England and Wales it seems that patients have rights but these rights have developed in an *ad hoc* manner and are difficult to identify. Nor are there very many. For example, there are rights under the Court of Protection and also under powers of attorney but these are limited to property and affairs. Other rights exist under guardianship. In England and Wales guardianship operates according to the 'essential powers' approach which means limiting the intervention of the guardian to matters of employment, and requiring the patient to attend for medical treatment but not enforcing it. In addition there are statute rights relating to hospital admissions or detention for assessment (under Section 136) when a patient can be detained for limited periods. There are also rights for elderly patients unable to look after themselves who can be detained under the National Assistance Act 1947. But there is little else. And those that exist do not address the questions we wish to ask here: i.e. do not address questions about receiving medication in the community, or about the possibility for that medication.

To illustrate this point about the lack of rights for people with mental health problems in the community most countries allow patients no explicit right to be discharged from hospital or to be given community treatment – though the modern claim that patients should be treated in the least restrictive alternative might perhaps cover that. Rarely, however, does one see legislation of the type contained in the Canadian North West Territories. This expressly states that a patient should be discharged from Mental Hospital when he is fit and able to assume his place in the community. Section 17(1) of that Mental Health Act says 'A patient shall be discharged from hospital when he is no longer in need of the observation, care or treatment provided therein.' It is interesting that most countries devise fairly elaborate rules relating to admission, and equally elaborate rules relating to treatment, but nothing about discharge. The physician is under no direct obligation to discharge a patient – perhaps because it is believed not to be necessary. Of course, patients rarely want to stay and physicians rarely want to keep them in hospital longer than required. But what is interesting about the Canadian legislation is that it places a direct obligation on the physician to do something, if only to focus attention on the patient's condition. (It could be argued that with the closure of mental hospitals the right to be readmitted or granted asylum is of greater importance than being discharged. Sometimes one thinks patients are discharged rather too quickly nowadays.)

But when contemplating community treatment the matter is complicated by the range of patients and the range of psychiatric conditions covered in the community. These are likely to be extensive – almost certainly wider then the range of patients in the mental hospital. There will be some with severe conditions, others with less severe conditions. There will be some patients with chronic conditions, some with acute states. Some patients will have prepared themselves for life in the community having anticipated their present position, others will not. Some will have good days and bad days, and some might have earlier secured powers of attorney and be prepared for community life. There will be others, such as the mentally impaired, whose condition has not changed nor is it likely to. All these patients have different demands for care. In this catalogue of patients some may require little or no care, some may require intermittent care and some may require permanent care and will continue to do so. In between there will be a host of other types and conditions with patients requiring assistance and having difficult expectations and demands.

Clearly different levels of treatment exist and have to be associated with different levels of responsibility. That means in turn that different levels of responsibility have to be associated with different sets of rights: the right to take decisions, the right to be regarded as capable of expressing certain views, or the right to refuse or accept treatment. Those providing treatment will have to vary their strategies of intervention, according to the different levels of responsibility of the patients – that is, those with little responsibility can expect greater levels of psychiatric intervention. One can see then that granting rights to patients becomes a complex process. It has to do with a mixture of the patients' psychiatric condition and the treatments provided. This of course presupposes that we know what is or should constitute psychiatric treatment, or how to distinguish between the treatment provided by a psychiatric team – whether a psychiatrist and social worker, or social worker and psychiatric nurse – from that given by the patient's family. It also presupposes that we know, and can determine what are the influences of the psychiatric treatment on the patient. As we shall see below psychiatric inputs are difficult to identify and equally difficult to measure. Negligence becomes more difficult to prove for patients in the community than for those in the hospital.

Treatments in the community

Assume that a patient is being treated in the community and assume too we know what constitutes treatment – say, the patient is having ECT or something similar, and that treatment goes wrong. The patient then sues for negligence. What then? Presumably there will be a test along the same lines as if the patient was in a hospital, whether mental hospital or other: tests are tests wherever they occur. The only question is, should the treatment setting be considered so different that it hinders the application of the test and makes it less relevant?

Immediately we ask this type of question we enter an uncharted area for there are no legal precedents on which to fall back and no rules or guidelines to use. In trying to assess the setting in which treatments take place we offer the following suggestions. On the face of it we suspect that the answer must be 'according to the type of treatments provided'. So if negligence is to be established where treatments have been given in the community it only matters whether the person who gave that treatment was shown to be negligent. Nothing else matters. Negligence is negligence under any circumstances, whenever and wherever it takes place. Patients – whether in the community or in hospital – are no different in this respect. Similarly, negligence exists if the quality of treatment is not up to standard. Again the community setting makes no difference. It matters not where the treatment took place or the negligence occurred for the same test would be applied.

Yet one can see how exemptions could be made or how an argument could be developed which says that the setting was critical. First the problem of treatment in the community is complicated by the lack of control the psychiatrist has over the patient and the psychiatrist's inability to control intervening variables. In mental hospitals patients receiving ECT (say) or powerful tranquillisers can be nursed in surroundings which can be controlled. Inappropriate behaviour can be monitored and checks introduced if required. There are few opportunities to do this in a community setting. The patient may leave the community clinic without medical or psychiatric support and so become more vulnerable than in hospital.

Second, it would be clear that patients given tranquillisers ought not to drive cars, nor work with heavy or dangerous machinery. Or patients receiving ECT ought not to be in situations where they need to remember things, and so on. Negligence assumes a different meaning when placed against the setting in which the patient lives and works. Options for treatment become reduced. Some courts have seen things this way. In the USA it is reported that because the courts recognise that psychiatrists lack significant control over out-patients recent decisions show a strong reluctance to impose liability. In one case, reported by Klein and Glover as *Speer* v. *US* 512 F. Supp. 67 (ND Tex, 1981), an out-patient overdosed on antipsychotic drugs prescribed by his psychiatrist. The court began by stating that the psychiatrists duty to out-patients is less extensive than the duty to in-patients (Klein and Glover, 1983, p. 148).

However, if the types of treatment provided were individual therapies, or group therapies, we think the results would be different. We say this because there are few tests able to show the direct impact of those therapies. Moreover, it is difficult to distinguish between therapy provided by the professional and the support and advice given by a friend or family. Negligence becomes much more difficult to prove here. The issue of causation – i.e. the relationship between treatment and the harm caused – is too imprecise to follow for reasonable decisions to be made. Injuries that are emotional rather than physical, we think will be less likely to be accepted, and less likely to be liable for negligence claims than those involving more direct treatments such as ECT or the use of neuroleptic drugs. But there will be grey areas where, although causation remains difficult to establish, it is still possible to say that one factor caused another. For example, a patient's condition may be aggravated or new injuries result – probably from negligent administration of medication – and in this case negligence would be proven.

To add a further level of complication: how are we to evaluate treatments given by the sector teams? If negligence occurs, which members of that team can be held responsible for it? Or will it be the whole team? Take the following example. Assume a patient has been referred by a GP and accepted for treatment. In line with current sector-team practice the patient may never see a psychiatrist or any physician for that matter. He may be treated by social workers or psychologists. Or he may be treated initially by a physician and then referred to a social worker who continues the treatment – using treatment in its widest sense. What are the patient's rights in such matters? What happens if the team social worker is professionally negligent in some way? Above all, how does a patient go about showing that negligence occurred in such circumstances i.e. show one member of the team was negligent rather than others?

Let us assume that a social worker engages in treatment that goes wrong. Assume also that the patient was referred to the team, allocated to a social worker by a team conference and was never seen by a psychiatrist. Could the psychiatrist who would normally claim to be the team leader be held responsible? In practice direct responsibility will lie with the Area Health Authority who are vicariously liable for their employees – in this case all members of the team, but that would still not get the psychiatrists off the hook. There would be no point in the patient suing the social worker who presumably has neither the personal nor professional means to cope with an award made against him/her. Nor would s/he be covered by an organisation such as the Medical Defence Union. Could the patient legitimately argue that it was the psychiatrist who was responsible ultimately and ought to have exercised more control over the social worker? There would be a distinct advantage for the patient to insist that negligence remains with the psychiatrist.

Of course all this is speculation, for until we know which direction the courts will take when confronted with such cases, we are without precedents or guidelines. But two clear questions remain. Are the courts likely to say that psychiatrists cannot be held responsible for patients treated in the community because patients are subject to varied influences impossible to determine? Or will they adopt a more radical approach and say that treatment must be given only after these factors have been taken into account? If past experience is anything to go on some court decisions will go one way, others another, before things begin to settle down. (There might even be judgements where, say, all members of sector teams are held liable – if so the effect would be profound). The track record of courts especially British ones suggests that they will err on the side of caution – and that does not mean on the side of the patient. The excuse will, we suspect, be that community treatments allow too many intervening variables for liability to be identified and defined. If that is to be so, the patient will lose out as before.

Patients' rights and the rights movement: an overview

Up to this point we have accepted that the promotion and preservation of rights is a good thing in itself. We have not sought to justify our position but have asserted in a self-evident way that the possession of rights enhances the dignity of the rights held and so exemplifies our idea of respect for persons (Campbell, 1988). In part we have regarded rights as self-evidently good because they place limits on the actions of others by restricting arbitrary power, and by protecting the individual from the cumulatively greater interests of others who may wish to exert influences or restrict freedom. In short, rights are self-evidently good because they protect the individual – collective and arbitrary powers being self-evidently bad.

Yet some have wanted to challenge that position whether by adopting a certain political stance or because they see rights as ineffective against the dominant power of psychiatry. A general critique of what is called rights-based-strategies would be as follows: the emphasis that rights place on the freedom of the individual may be seen as a real hindrance to the achievement of the sort of equalitarian and welfare-oriented society which is a prime goal of social justice. Rights give individuals unreasonable powers of veto over important social objectives. With its emphasis on individual choice and the liberty of the individual the theory of rights turns out to be an ideologically partisan theory in which liberties are favoured disproportionately over equality (Campbell, 1988, p. 38). So rights are part of a political strategy emphasised by liberal capitalist type societies where freedom of the individual is considered important. They are derided by those who favour a more collective stance, for rights allow the individual to stand against and hold up progress of that collective. We do not propose to defend or attack that argument for that would be to enter another debate altogether different in tone and character. We do however wish to accept the point made above: political positions are bound up in theory of rights.

A second type of argument aims at criticising rights-based strategies, not necessarily for what they stand for, but for what they avoid and cover up. This position is advanced by Nicolas Rose who states that rights and their attendant links with legalism do not reflect the nature of decisions made by psychiatrists nor do they provide effective monitoring. Nor do they constrain psychiatric discretion. They tend only to bring about a shift in the topics of discussion and the personnel involved. In one passage Rose puts the argument thus:

> Rights-based strategies are not effective in the calculation of priorities or the resolution of conflicts for conceptualising or defending freedoms, for characterising or evaluating decision-making processes, for regulating or improving them or for analysing or transforming the powers of expertise over those subject to it. It sidesteps the ethical issues by smuggling in an unanalysed morality concerning the values and antecedents of humans and the rule of just conduct. It evades the political

issues by its inability to confront the question of the distribution of scarce resources amongst priorities and by disguising the politics of its own utilization of legal mechanisms for the exercise of political power (Rose, 1986).

There is much wrong with this yet much, too, that is interesting. What is wrong is that it grossly overstates the case. The Mental Health Act 1983 came after the British Government was censured by the European Court for its failure to protect patients' rights. Rights enacted by that Act may be less than required but they were better than those previously recognised and were a significant advance in terms of protecting the patients against arbitrary powers. And if not that strategy what else? We agree with Philip Fennell (1986) who says 'when reminded by Rose of the limited nature of law and legal mechanisms *vis-à-vis* other mechanisms of organising monitoring and transforming social provision we are entitled to ask what these other provisions are before baby and bathwater disappear together'. To say, too, as Rose does, that rights evade political issues and disguise the politics of its own utilisation, or that rights sidestep ethical issues by smuggling in an unanalysed morality concerning the value and attributes of humans and the role of just conduct, is simply wrong.

The right to privacy, for example, if granted would stand for a precise ethical issue, a clear morality and a role of just conduct. Privacy is about respect for persons' right to be dealt with in this or that way (moral) and about the right not to have areas of freedom infringed (political).

Yet what is interesting about Rose's statement is that he draws attention to the limits of rights-based strategies. And indeed there are clear limits. If rights are to be valued they must be granted and be capable of being enforced. That depends on the integrity and willingness of numerous people in organisations, not least the courts, who are required to impose and interpret the law as favourable to rights. Sometimes we have looked in vain for the courts to do just that. They have not always protected the citizen against the powers of the state in mental health matters.

What is also correct about Rose's view is that rights are blunt instruments. It is better to improve levels of practice than have to rely on legally interpreted statutes. Practices which are sensitive and of good quality must surely be the aim. Regulation by internal mechanisms using the powers of institutions or offering professional prescriptions against offending is also superior to heavy-handed legislation. All this is clear. But what happens when such mechanisms fail? Rights, the courts and litigation are all that is left. Hence Fennell's comments that we must be wary lest babies and bath water disappear together (see also Bingley, 1985).

7
Discharge of Mentally Disordered Offenders

In this chapter we want to describe the position of the mentally abnormal offender, one of the key casualties of the decarceration movement. Mentally abnormal offenders provide another piece to the jigsaw and their position is increasingly precarious. Offenders, once able to find sanctuary in the mental hospitals, are now ending up in the penal system. In this chapter we wish to show how the mentally abnormal offender fares under decarceration and the problems associated with transferring such offenders out of the penal system into the mental health services.

The mentally abnormal offender in the prison system

Not all mentally disordered patients are in mental hospitals: many remain elsewhere, such as in prisons where they may receive little or no psychiatric attention. At the end of their sentence they will be discharged, perhaps going through the so-called 'revolving door': they will leave prison, but may find themselves admitted to a mental hospital – that is, if a place is available. On leaving the hospital they could be readmitted to the prison: and so on and so on. At least that was what happened a decade or so ago but with the run-down of the mental hospitals, one part of that revolving door has been closed. Prisons have now become the key institutions for the containment of the mentally disordered. They act as major service-providers but, as we shall see later, accept that role somewhat reluctantly.

Yet having said that the prison is the paramount service provided for the mentally disabled offender and it is by no means clear how many mentally disordered people are in them. Estimates vary enormously. At one extreme there are data from the prison medical services showing about 300 mentally disordered in prisons in England and Wales in 1988; at the other, estimates put the figure at about 16 000. It is not easy to see why such variations occur or pick ones way through the differing arguments.

Consider first that estimate from the prison medical officers. Table 7.1 provides data for a 10-year period taken from the annual returns to the Home Office by prison medical officers.

Not only is the aggregate small but the trend is downward – apart from increases in 1986 and 1987 which have been interpreted by the Home Office as no more than a short-term deflection from an otherwise longer downward trend. The figures include sentenced and unsentenced prisoners alike. In 1986, for example, of the 333 prisoners described as suffering from mental disorder, 137 were sentenced, 196 were unsentenced prisoners.

At the other extreme prisons are seen as taking more and more people who would otherwise have gone into the mental hospital system. Indeed some commentators suggest that about one third of all prisoners, sentenced and unsentenced, could be regarded as mentally disordered – i.e. in England and Wales. On the basis of the current prison population that would be about 16 000 prisoners. This figure of 16 000 is regarded by the Home Office as a 'bench-mark' which is a polite way of calling it an inspired guess. And one can see why the Home Office remains sceptical: the

Table 7.1 *Mentally disordered prisoners in 1977–88*

Year	Number
1977	759
1978	581
1979	557
1980	457
1981	320
1982	282
1983	316
1984	283
1985	251
1986	333
1987	354
1988	290

Source: Interdepartmental Working Group of the Home Office, 1988.

search for the true prevalence has proven difficult. The main problem is, as always, one of definition. Some studies include only those prisoners who could be detained under the Mental Health Act 1983, others use a wider definition. Some have included drug addicts and alcoholics; others only those who are psychotic. And others, which include those returns by the prison medical officers, have tended to define 'mentally disordered' as being only those with a reasonable chance of being accepted for treatment in the mental hospitals outside. Somewhat naturally this excludes the chronic patients, the disruptive and the violent.

That so called 'benchmark' of 30 per cent came originally from a study by John Gunn in 1977 of sentenced male prisoners in south-east region (Gunn, 1977, para. 5.2). It fits in with data from a Canadian study of Federal prisoners where 3 per cent were estimated to have a psychiatric problem and a further 25 per cent to have a psychiatric disorder. (Even then some Canadian psychiatrists regarded that figure as a little on the low side because it did not include prisoners addicted to alcohol.) But both figures are widely different from data provided by the Directorate of Prison Medical Services in England and Wales as shown in Tables 7.2 and 7.3. The data were taken from a snapshot census of mentally disturbed prisoners by medical officers on 4 December 1988. An earlier census was undertaken on 1 October 1986. Both were for sentenced prisoners: the main purpose being said to be managerial. The Home Office claimed that 'surveys of this nature which call on the individual clinical judgement of the medical officer of a large number of establishments would produce results perhaps best taken as illustrative of the scale involved' (Home Office, 1987, Annex C, para. 5:5).

Five points can be made from these tables:

1. the definitions used were generally speaking based on those of Section 1 of the 1983 Mental Health Act – except for 'personality disorder' which is not defined by the Act.
2. 'personality disorder' was defined broadly as covering a range of less seriously disturbed inmates. It included those who manifest exaggerated personality symptoms whether aggression or withdrawal – but as is usual in these matters it remains unclear, which criteria were used.
3. the data show the largest group of mentally disordered offenders to be those suffering from personality disorder (in fact over 60 per cent of the whole group) with relatively few suffering from mental illness. So, for example, in 1986, 941 of

Table 7.2 *Extract from census of mentally disturbed male prisoners undertaken by medical officers on 4 December 1985 and 1 October 1986*

	Mental illness		Sense impairment		Mental impairment		Psychopathic disorder		Personality disorder		Total	
	1985	1986	1985	1986	1985	1986	1985	1986	1985	1986	1985	1986
Adult	281	233	3	–	45	82	211	174	720	941	1260	1430
Young offender	12	17	–	–	26	34	16	26	183	242	237	319
Total	293	250	3	–	71	116	227	200	903	1183	1497	1749

Source: Interdepartmental working group of Home Office and DHSS officials on mentally disturbed offenders in the prison system in England and Wales (Home Office, 1987, Annex C, p. 27). Acknowledgement is made for permission to reproduce this and Tables 7.1, 7.2, 7.3 and 7.4.

Table 7.3 *Percentage of mentally disturbed prisoners in male prison population, grouped according to the length of sentence*

	6 months		Over 6 months up to 12 months		Over 12 months up to 5 years		Over 5 years		Life		Total	
	1985	1986	1985	1986	1985	1986	1985	1986	1985	1986	1985	1986
Adults	2.71	4.09	2.71	3.3	3.53	4.74	9.2	9.68	14.19	14.89	5.11	5.9
Young offender	1.86	2.46	1.93	2.95	3.99	4.45	12.05	17.29	29.07	50.59	3.60	4.4
Mean	2.41	3.47	2.43	3.17	3.62	4.68	9.32	9.99	14.79	16.39	4.79	5.5

Source: As for Table 7.2.

the 1430 adult inmates in the whole year were regarded as having a personality disorder.

4. in Table 7.3 the highest percentage of mentally disordered as a percentage of the male prison population were amongst the life sentences, particularly the young offenders. (50.59 per cent of young offenders in 1986). In contrast only 2.71 per cent of adults serving sentences of 6 months or less in 1985, and 4.09 per cent in 1986 were seen to be mentally disordered – we say surprisingly because many commentators have suggested that mental disorder would be highest amongst the short sentenced group who would be expected to include the petty inadequate itinerant offenders.

5. the total numbers listed, whilst not as high as the 30 per cent 'bench-mark', are considerably higher than those of the prison medical officers in Table 7.1.

Differences between the data from the various surveys listed above are not easy to reconcile. To complicate matters further, Washbrook conducted three surveys at intervals of 6–7 months in Winson Green prison Birmingham. He studied 600 prisoners, all sentenced, and found 11.6 per cent, 7.5 per cent and 8.6 per cent respectively in need of psychiatric care – with an average of 9.25 per cent (Washbrook, 1977). Similarly in a survey of Brixton prison about 9 per cent of the inmates were classified as psychotic (see Smith, 1984) but Brixton is a local remand prison and may be unrepresentative of prisons generally. And, to complicate matters even further, Coid, in his study, spoke of only 1 per cent of sentenced prisoners being psychotic (Coid, 1984) with proportionate levels of psychosis no higher than in the general population. This in contrast to some North American studies which show a higher proportion of psychotic prisoners: 5 per cent classified as schizophrenic, or 5.9 per cent as having *dementia praecox* in Sing Sing (quoted in Coid, 1984).

Again part of the explanation can be found in matters of definition – the American studies seem to use a more generous definition of schizophrenia than is general in the UK. Also there are questions of diagnostic reliability: Washbrook, for example, (1987) gives no evidence to show how he made his diagnosis, nor does Gunn, nor do the prison medical officers in the survey listed above. Yet in spite of the disagreements there are some important agreements too: most prison studies seem to show high numbers of people with psychopathic and personality disorders in their populations, and most show a small but persistent group of mentally impaired prisoners. Similarly, most show some over-representation of epileptic prisoners. However, for a more definitive statement we now have a newly commissioned Home Office Study on the mentally disordered in British prisons. This was aimed at producing a psychiatric profile of the prison population in England and Wales and an assessment of facilities on which policy considerations may be based in the next decade. Results show 38.8 per cent as the estimated prevalence of psychiatric disorder amongst all sentenced prisoners (Gunn *et al.*, 1991).

Transfer, treatment or discharge

But there still remains the problem of what to do with these mentally disordered offenders. Should they be treated within the prison system and do they have a right to such treatment? The latter question raises interesting problems. In Canadian prisons for example, the possibility of receiving treatment affects the prisoner's release date. Prisoners classified as mentally disordered will not get parole unless they have received appropriate treatment for their condition. For these prisoners treatment would have to be provided as of right: failure to provide it could be discriminatory. Similarly in some states in the USA untreated prisoners claim they are subject to 'cruel and unusual punishment' if treatment is not provided. So in the USA or rather in parts of the USA where facilities and money are available, prisoners claim they have a right to treatment. In Britain, and Canada, things are less clear-cut. Prisoners have a common-law right to health-service facilities but that may not be enforceable – at least not yet, though one can see how it could be in the future.

Yet if treatment is provided, and one can easily accept the common-law view that it should, there remains the tricky question as to where it should be given. In the prison perhaps? Or somewhere else? If not in prison, then perhaps a mental hospital? If so there must be procedures able to promote and deal with transfers from the prisons to the hospitals. There must also be a process whereby those requiring treatment are efficiently identified. That could mean a greatly enlarged prison medical/psychiatric system. If not, then why not concentrate on developing an adequate mental hospital system – adequate to take offenders and adequate to treat them. Of course no such mental hospital system exists, at least in Britain, nor anywhere else which has promoted decarceration. This is what we mean when we say that the mentally disturbed offenders are one of the major casualties of the present system.

Provisions for transfers

As things stand there are provisions under the Mental Health Act 1983 for prisoners diagnosed as mentally disordered to transfer to mental hospitals, or to Special Hospitals if they are considered dangerous and by Special Hospitals we mean those hospitals which provide high levels of security who will take, *inter alia* the criminally insane. All patients sent to Special Hospitals must meet certain legal criteria, and there must be a place available for them. Here we meet another insurmountable problem, which has predated any problem created by the run-down of the mental hospitals. As far as the ordinary mental hospitals are concerned they are not – and have never been – keen to take offender patients.

Nor does it seem that the Special Hospitals are keen either, especially those considered chronic, long-stay or intractable, and even less so if the patients are diagnosed as mentally impaired or psychopathic.

The legal requirements for the transfer of patients from prisons in England and Wales are set out in part III of the 1983 Act. Briefly, the Home Secretary can (under Section 47) direct that a person serving a sentence of imprisonment or other forms of detention be removed to and detained in a hospital. Elsewhere, Section 48 empowers the Home Secretary to direct the removal from prison to hospital of certain categories of mentally disordered persons and of unsentenced prisoners. Where an unsentenced prisoner's condition is such that immediate removal to a hospital is necessary, then, when the prisoner is well enough, he is either produced at court from hospital or returned to prison to await trial). There are also powers for the Home Secretary to impose restrictions on persons transferred, e.g. they cannot be transferred to another hospital, sent on leave or discharged without his consent. (See Jones, 1983 for a more detailed discussion on these legal matters.)

It can be seen from Table 7.4 that the numbers of sentenced prisoners transferred remain small – about 100 per year, with half as many again in the unsentenced category. Table 7.4 also gives data on all prisoners, sentenced and unsentenced alike, transferred between 1978 and 1986. Section 47 of the Act relates to sentenced prisoners, Section 48 to unsentenced ones.

The main point from this table is that there has been a steady increase of transferred sentenced prisoners, i.e. almost 100 per

Table 7.4 *Transfers from prison to hospital under Sections 47 and 48 of the 1983 Mental Health Act*

	1978	1979	1980	1981	1982	1983	1984	1985	1986
Sect. 47*	53	84	87	86	85	92	108	100	104
Sect. 48*	9	16	19	22	18	23	47	41	45
Total	62	100	106	108	103	115	155	141	149

* or equivalent under the 1959 Act.

Source: HMSO (1987) Interdepartmental working group of Home Office and DHSS officials on mentally disordered offenders: the prison system in England and Wales.

cent increase in 1986 over 1978. There is an even greater increase of transfers for unsentenced prisoners in the same decade under review – about 400 per cent.

Welcome though they might be these figures have to be seen in perspective. The aggregate remains small: 149 in 1986 out of a prison population approaching 50 000. Moreover the proportion has declined. Sir Lionel Fox, for example, reporting in 1931, when the average prison population was about 12 000 noted that 105 sentenced prisoners were transferred to mental hospitals in that year. (There were 98 convicted prisoners certified as insane from the local prisons with 7 more from the convict prisons. In addition 47 others were transferred: 45 from local prisons classified as mentally defective, and another 2 from convict prisons (Orr, 1978).)

Sir Lionel Fox thought the justification for transfer abundantly clear. He regarded it as self-evident that prison was not the place for an offender who was either insane or mentally defective (using the terminology of the old Lunacy and Mental Deficiency Acts). He expected that most insane prisoners would be identified at the remand stage, though there might be a few who slipped through the net or later became insane during their sentence. (There remains the difficult but intriguing question as to what extent the patients/prisoner's mental disorder occurred as a result of the sentence rather than being brought with him into the prison. We are not concerned with that question here as it has only marginal relevance to questions of transfer or discharge but we wonder how many offenders are made mentally disturbed by the prison system.) Sir Lionel Fox put it this way:

> Considerable advances have been made since the war [that is, the 1914–18 war] in the treatment of problems connected with mental disease among prisoners: indeed it would seem that today the investigation and recognition of mental states . . . have come to form the most important part of the medical officers duties (Sir L. Fox, quoted in Orr, 1978, p. 195).

Sir Lionel like many others after him might argue that transfers were self-evidently good. Yet given the small numbers involved he might suspect that there was something amiss with the procedures. Clearly there are differences between the assessments of the numbers of mentally disordered by outside researchers and those of the prison medical service. Even so, how is it that so few prisoners are transferred? That question begs an earlier one and presupposes that Sir Lionel Fox was correct in his assumption that offenders with mental health problems ought to be transferred. Some prisoners would dispute this, preferring to serve their sentence in prison and be certain of discharge rather than be let out when they are considered cured. Whether so or not, the prison service seems doubly disadvantaged. It does not transfer patients who are mentally disordered, and with the closure of the mental hospitals will be expected to take more of them.

Provisions for sentence and transfer

The debate about transfers has been long and acrimonious. It is tied into a second and related debate about sentencing the mentally abnormal offender to a hospital order.

The hospital order is a peculiarly British 'sentence', absent in North America, yet not without its supporters who see the advantages of being able to order offenders to be treated in hospital. The legal requirement for making a hospital order comes from Section 37 of the 1983 Act (equivalent to Section 60 of the 1959 Act). Powers to make a hospital order are limited to offenders normally punishable by a prison sentence – except where the sentence is fixed by law, as with murder. The Hospital Order lasts initially for 6 months requiring renewal by the Responsible Medical Officer (RMO) after a further 6 months, and thereafter annually. The RMO however may discharge the patient at his discretion. The grounds for making a hospital order are similar to those for Section 3: the offender must be suffering from mental illness, mental impairment, severe mental impairment, or psychopathic disorder, which must be of a nature and degree which makes it appropriate for him to be detained in hospital. In the case of psychopathic disorder such treatment should be likely to alleviate or prevent deterioration of his condition – this has been inserted to stop the hospital order being used simply as an alternative to prison.

The Court of Appeal has held that the imposition of a hospital order should depend on the present mental state of the offender and not on the degree of criminal responsibility at the time the offender was committed. It is not necessary therefore to establish a causal connection between the offender's mental condition and the offence before a hospital order can be made (Verdun-Jones, 1989). Offenders on a hospital order may be sent to a local psychiatric hospital, a Regional Secure Unit providing a greater measure of security, or one of the four Special Hospitals which provide beds to those considered to be a serious risk to the public. When a hospital order is made by the Crown Court – not a magistrates' court – a Restriction Order may be made in addition to Section 37. (There will be a more detailed discussion of Restriction Orders later.) The judge making a Restriction Order will do so on the basis that it is necessary to protect the public from serious harm. The Order may be for an unlimited time or for a specified period. Patients on a Restriction Order may not be granted leave, transferred or discharged without consent of the Home Secretary. The RMO is required to send periodic reports to the Home Secretary on each patient. Patients are usually admitted to Special Hospitals but may be admitted or later transferred to ordinary mental hospitals with the approval of the Home Secretary if a hospital is willing to secure the patient.

This briefly is the legal requirement for the hospital order and its companion, the Restriction Order. Hospital Orders provide a psychiatric alternative to the prison system. They are, or should be, imposed for the explicit purpose of treatment rather than punishment – although the courts tend to produce rather curious reasons when they have to consider whether a hospital order could be seen as a sentence of greater severity than (say) one of a short term of imprisonment. The hospital order places the patient in the hands of the doctors, forgoing any question of punishment, and relinquishing from then on the court's control over the patient, whether for treatment or discharge. It may well be that hospital orders have led to the offender spending a longer period in custody, albeit in a hospital, than would have occurred had the offender been sent to prison – and almost certainly if a Restriction Order was imposed. Even so, the Court of Appeal has held that courts must not consider this: what matters is that the offender will be given treatment.

We do not wish to get too embroiled in a detailed discussion of hospital orders generally or Restriction Orders in particular, for it is not so much entry via those Orders which are of interest as the methods by which patients are able to get out of the Hospital Regional Secure Unit, or the Special Hospital. There are two reasons for including such matters here:

1. discharges from special Hospitals and Regional Secure Units are part of the problem of discharges generally;
2. the problem of entry into the hospital order is related to the problem of transfers from the prison.

Those problems can be crystalised under two headings:

1. reluctance to accept such patients in the hospital;
2. the decline more recently in the number of hospital places available.

In the former heading there is a long history of antagonism between the hospitals, the prisons and the courts. Prisons and courts have been keen to get offender patients into the hospitals but the hospitals have not been willing to take them. That the hospitals have a choice is regarded by some, including many lawyers and social scientists, as beyond belief: few other countries allow the medical profession such unbridled latitude. But a choice they have, and that choice is written into the legislation. The 1983 Act requires that a place must be available to a patient before the court can make the order (Section 37). Walker and McCabe say:

> Since the number of prisoners remanded for psychiatric examination is about four times as high as the numbers made subject of hospital orders, or psychiatric probation orders, it is clear that prison medical officers and their colleagues whom they call in from mental hospitals for consultation, could, if minded, receive many more hospital orders than they in fact do (Walker and McCabe, 1973).

The essence of the debate, whether of transfers from prisons to hospital, or of the provision of the court to make a hospital order, has centred on the powers granted to the medical profession to agree to receive the patient in hospital. Section 37(a) says in respect of a hospital order that:

> An order for the admission of an offender to a hospital shall not be made . . . unless the court is satisfied in the written or oral evidence of the RMO . . . that arrangements have been made for his admission . . . For transfer to hospital from prison there is no comparable subsection in the Act giving a requirement for the consent of the receiving hospital to be obtained but in practice the Home Secretary seeks consent before directing transfers from prison (Jones, 1983).

In both cases the hospitals must have places for them and must agree to take them.

That the hospitals do not agree has been a bone of contention for years. In 1976 the Butler Committee considered the matter, sympathised with all parties concerned yet avoided a direct conclusion. It said 'the problem of the mentally abnormal prisoner was to be tackled with urgency, determination and a massive injection of money' (HMSO, 1975). Nothing has happened. Some have seen the problem centring around the provision of services. The legal correspondent of the *BMJ* put it this way. 'The options given to the court may therefore be limited if facilities are not available, as they frequently are not for people who are not so mentally ill as to qualify for a Special Hospital' (*BMJ*, 9 Feb 1985, p. 447). Others see the problem as being associated with the powers of nursing staff who according to Robert Bluglass, have lost their skills to care for difficult and disturbed patients because of the open-door policy in mental hospitals (quoted in Orr), yet the All-Party Parliamentary Group on Mental Health put the matter differently. They suggested that much could be achieved by improving staffing and facilities in ordinary mental hospitals and emphasised the need for flexibility of movement between psychiatric hospitals and the community, the focal point being the mental hospital (quoted in Bluglass, 1978, vol. 1, p. 489). Still others, such as the legal correspondent of the *BMJ* puts the blame back on the Government. It noted that the Butler Committee recommended that a special verdict of 'not guilty on evidence of mental disorder' should be returned if the court were satisfied that at the time the offence was committee the accused was suffering from mental disorder.

> If the law was changed in that way and actually applied in practice to all offices, the prison population would be appreciably reduced and the number of people sent to hospital under court order would be increased by an equal number. Many prisoners are so disordered mentally that they ought to be in hospital. If the Butler proposals had been implemented they would have been acquitted and could not be sent to prison (*British Medicine Journal*, 9 February 1985, vol. 290, p. 447).

Whatever the perceived cause of the problem, nothing seems to have been done to ease it. Psychiatrists argue that the mental hospitals ought not to be regarded as the old-style asylum. Orr says 'Hospitals have clearly sought to divest themselves of the traditional role of providing asylum for people unable to cope elsewhere even if there is no specific treatment for their condition such as to ameliorate it or prevent it from getting worse.' (Orr, 1978, p. 196). Psychiatrists clearly have no wish to return to earlier security and prison-like conditions and regard an influx of pa-

tients requiring that level of control as being a retrograde step.
They say, with some truth, that they are the best judges of patients
requiring treatment. They add that it makes no sense to fill the
hospitals with untreatable patients merely as a way of avoiding
prison overcrowding. That may be so, but might it not be a won-
derful excuse to avoid taking this type of patient?

The Home Office Select Committee certainly saw things that
way. In 1980 it recommended that legislation should be introduced to force Regional Health Authorities to take prisoners when
the court made a Hospital Order (HMSO, 1981, The Prison Service, 4th Report). No such legislation was introduced though
Section 39 of the 1983 Mental Health Act, was a compromise
aimed at easing matters. It stated that whenever a court was
considering making a hospital order, it should ask the appropriate health authority to provide information as to the availability
of suitable hospital places. This, as far as can be seen, has not
improved matters greatly, if at all. However, we wonder what
will happen in the light of the current movement towards hospitals opting out of the NHS and preparing for consequent pricing
of services. In some areas of the country new pressures are being
brought to bear on mental hospitals to take patients ready to leave
Special Hospitals. Payments for costs incurred in keeping these
patients in Special Hospitals are being demanded by them to
retain patients waiting to return to their districts of residence. We
wonder what effects this financial consideration will have on
future Mental Hospital policy in respect of Special Hospital inmates since April 1991, when charging for services has become
fully operational. These pressures have to be balanced against
competing ones, i.e. those genuine clinical emergencies, and the
transfers of prisoners from prison to hospital on orders awaiting
medical reports under the Mental Health Act which have to be
complied with within 28 days of their implementation.

Of course the absence of hospital places and the closure of
mental hospitals has proceeded at an awesome pace in the 1980's
with, we suspect, little consideration given to the plight of the
mentally abnormal offenders. They were the last to be acknow-
ledged in the overall scheme of things. Yet the consequences are
becoming clear: some cities in England and Wales will have no
mental hospitals at all by the mid-1990s. Where can the mentally
abnormal offenders then go? The only possibilities are new purpose-built accommodation, hostels, etc. or Regional Secure Units.
But as we show later, there are few places available and little

prospect of there being any. The other option is for the offenders to remain where they are – and that means in prison, though with the demand to reduce the prison population even the prisons could be closed down. That could leave the community: in which case we are back to where we started, the whole system is on a never-ending roller-coaster.

The special problem of the Special Hospitals

Discharges from Special Hospitals pose their own unique problems. For those involved in the process, the aim is often a pragmatic one: to get the patients out of the Special Hospitals, even if it means transferring them to another secure institution; to a Regional Secure Unit perhaps or an ordinary mental hospital. Rarely are patients discharged from a Special Hospital direct to the community.

Before we look at the problems of getting out of the Special Hospital we need to consider some of the legal requirements for entry. This gives an idea of the types of patients with whom we are dealing and the problems they pose. No one suggests that discharge from the Special Hospital is, or ought to, be a routine matter. Special Hospitals take some of the most intractable patients and are the 'end of the line', as it were. But we are suggesting that a mixture of professional dominance, and extreme caution – in what proportion we do not know – seem to conspire to reduce the number of patients discharged. That means that some are detained under more severe restrictions than they need – which, if nothing else, is an attack on their rights to be placed in facilities no more severe than necessary.

For legal purposes two conditions must apply for all patients admitted to Special Hospitals, irrespective of their source:

1. there must be present a form of mental disorder, of a nature or degree which qualifies the patient for compulsory treatment under the Mental Health Act;
2. the patient must be considered dangerous or violent of a nature or degree which requires conditions of security.

The legislation is enabling rather than directive, allowing discretion at various stages of the admission process (Chiswick, 1982, p. 131). These hospitals are the direct responsibility of the Department of Health. Under the National Health Service

Reorganisation Act 1972, Special Hospitals are for persons who in the opinion of the Secretary of State 'require treatment under conditions of special security on account of their dangerous, violent or criminal propensities'.

Entrance to the Special Hospitals is by a number of routes: either through the courts after an offence has been committed (about 30 per cent) or from the prison (about 6 per cent), or from psychiatric hospitals or hospitals for the subnormal or mentally impaired (about 63 per cent). Rarely are admissions direct from the community. About 25 per cent of all patients admitted are women. There were about 240 patients admitted in 1981. This figure had dropped to 184 by 1988. About 300 patients leave each year – this imbalance is of recent origin and it means that the Special Hospital population is on the decline.

The Mental Health Act 1983 empowers a Crown Court, but not a Magistrates' Court when making a hospital order, to make a Restriction Order. Orders restricting a discharge may be made under Section 41, and only when a hospital order is made, i.e. not a Guardianship Order. Restriction orders may be either for a specified period or without limit of time. Under Section 42(1) they may be terminated at any time by the Home Secretary.

There are two main methods for the discharge of patients in Special Hospitals;

1. through the powers of the Home Secretary if the patient is on a Restriction Order;
2. through a Mental Health Review Tribunal (MHRT); though this simplifies a complex process as MHRTs advise the Home Secretary on the discharge of all Restricted patients

Even so, and for these purposes it is best to see discharges from the Special Hospitals as coming through two main routes. We shall deal first and briefly with the Home Secretary's powers on a Restriction Order, later discharges through the Mental Health review Tribunal.

When a patient is admitted to hospital on a Restriction Order he may not be given leave of absence or be transferred to another hospital or be discharged except with the Home Secretary's consent. (He may however apply to a MHRT, but see below). Under Section 41(6) the responsible medical officer (RMO) has a duty to keep continually under review the suitability for discharge of all patients who are subject to a restriction order and he is obliged to report at least annually to the Home Secretary on each restricted patient in his care. The DHSS say the initiative in seeking the Home Secretary's consent to discharge lies with the RMO and the managers who should not hesitate to seek permission when they consider a patient's condition warrants it. Moreover, says the Department of Health, hospital managers should not assume that consent to discharge will not be given before the end of the period named in a Restriction Order since the Home Secretary has discretion to discharge at any time (DHSS Memorandum to Parts I to VI, VIII and X of the Mental Health Act, 1983, para. 163).

The proportion of patients on Restriction Orders is large – 877 out of a total of 1732 or about 50 per cent (Special Hospital Patient Statistics, 1988, DH Table 3A). The manner in which the Home Secretary reaches his decision to discharge Restricted patients is not made public and the patient has no right of appeal (Chiswick, 1982, p. 131). We are told that the decision is related to the Home Secretary's 'responsibility for the protection of the public to refuse or postpone his consent to discharge' but nothing more is known. Some public details, information and guidelines on this seem long overdue.

The second method of discharge is by the decision of the Mental Health Review Tribunals – though matters are more complicated when the patient is on a Restriction Order (see Sections 72 and 73 of the 1983 Act). As the MHRTs are the main source of discharge we shall look at these in greater detail.

The Royal Commission, the Percy Commission in 1957 introduced the tribunal system and MHRTs were then introduced under the 1959 Mental Health Act. The Aarvold Committee summarised their role as being 'a safeguard for the liberty of the individual and to ensure against unjustified detention in hospital' (Aarvold Report, 1973, para. 35). RM Jones says that the Commission proposed that reviews should be undertaken by a local tribunal which would consist of medical and non-medical members selected from a panel of suitable people. (Jones, 1983). However, Jill Peay makes the point about this effectiveness, or rather lack of it. She says:

> Research into the working of the Tribunals under the 1959 Act resulted in widespread criticism both of their methods and of the deficits inherent in the system. Their powers and procedures were criticised: inconsistency was demonstrated in their decisions; and the legal criteria which were supposed to govern their decisions were found either to be routinely outweighed by other non-legal criteria or,

more worryingly, to be misapplied or ignored. Despite the consensus basis of tribunal decision-making drawing on legal, psychiatric and lay expertise, differences between individual tribunal members attitudes towards and knowledge about mental health issues were found to have a systematic effect on the decisions made. Although tribunal members could and did apply the law comparatively, their decision could be characterised neither as just nor efficacious. The tribunal system was fundamentally flawed and the impetus for reform overwhelming (Peay, 1988).

Strong stuff indeed. The Mental Health Act 1983 has been intended to meet some of those features. Substantial changes had been made in the nature of the tribunal, strengthening and changing them. For example, changes had been made in the type of patients eligible to apply for hearings: 'patients who do not exercise their rights to a tribunal hearing shall have their cases referred automatically by the hospital managers every three years' thus 'ensuring that patients who also lack the ability or initiative to make an application to a Tribunal . . . have the safeguard of an independent review of the case' (quoted in Jones, 1983) The membership of panels dealing with Restricted cases has also been changed. Tribunals dealing with Restricted cases are now chaired by a Circuit Judge or Recorder being 'a person with substantial judicial experience in the criminal courts' (see Parliamentary Debates, Lords, col. 761, 25 January 1982). More specifically in Restricted cases tribunals have powers to discharge a patient, and indeed are obliged to discharge a patient if they are satisfied that the patient is not then suffering from one of the four specified mental disorders or from 'any of those forms of disorder of a nature or degree which makes it appropriate for him to be liable to be detained in a hospital for medical treatment'. Or if they are satisfied that 'it is not necessary for the health or safety of the patient or for the protection of other persons that he should receive such treatment (Section 72 (6)(ii) and Section 73).

In addition Restricted patients must meet new conditions of 'treatability' and 'viability':

the Tribunal shall have regard to the likelihood of medical treatment alleviating or preventing a deterioration of the patients condition, and in the case of a patient suffering from mental illness or severe mental impairment to the likelihood of the patient, if discharged being able to care for himself, to obtain the care he needs or to guard himself against serious exploitation (Mental Health Act, 1983, Section 72(2)(a)(b)).

These were introduced into the 1983 Act to counterbalance the dominance of medical criteria. Jill Peay says: 'Their behavioural basis was intended to permit non-medical people to have a greater say in determining the necessary for compulsory treatment' (Peay, 1988).

One of the few pieces of extensive research conducted on MHRTs to identify the manner in which MHRTs discharged or recommended discharge of patients, was conducted by Jill Peay in 1988. Her results are alarming.

First, dealing with the Tribunals duty to act as a 'safeguard of an independent review of the case', she found that of the 94 determined cases the MHRTs made decisions to discharge in 18 of these, and decisions for transfer or trial leave in a further 16, but mostly (60 out of 94) they made neither a decision to discharge nor any recommendation for change in a patient's status. More importantly the Tribunal followed the advice offered to them by the RMO in 81 cases, or 86 per cent of the sample, suggesting, as others have found in studies of Tribunals, that Tribunals ratify rather than make decisions. But there is worse to come. In 11 of the 13 cases when the Tribunal rejected the RMOs advice, they reached decisions which were more cautious than advocated by the RMO. Or put another way: patients would have been more likely to gain greater levels of freedom had the Tribunal system not operated. And have the changes in the compositions of the Tribunal affected things? Apparently not very much. Jill Peay says:

> Judicial members were reluctant to go against the advice they were offered by the RMO: generally they believed that since the RMO knew the patient best his view was critical. In those cases when they rejected his advice, the judicial members stated that this was most likely to be because the RMO was proposing an unjustifiably risky course of action (Peay, 1988).

This is a slightly different form of professional dominance than discussed hitherto, but occurs where professionals take or rely on other professionals' decisions. Do the RMOs really know best, and did they really know the patient well enough to make those judgements? It depends on one's expectations. Patients, it seems, drew attention to the very low level of contact with the RMOs: on average patients saw their RMOs once every 4 months. Not surprisingly most patients felt that the RMOs had a poor understanding of them as people or of their case. Indeed some patients applied for tribunal hearings for reasons other than seeking their discharge. The reason most frequently cited was 'to find out about the progress of their case': or as Jill Peay puts it: 'Patients are aware that one of the surest ways to obtain a formal interview with the RMO was apply for a Tribunal hearing' (Peay, 1988). And when the RMOs did not like what they heard from the Tribunal what then? Jill Peay reports a further alarming and disturbing finding:

> Where the tribunal made recommendations which the RMO opposed most of them stated that they would either take no action to enforce the recommendations or that they would make it plain – for example, to the hospital where the patient might have been recommended for transfer – that they, the RMOs, opposed such a move. This effectively prevented a bed being offered. Only one RMO said he was happy to look for an alternative placement if directed to do so by a Tribunal (Peay, 1988).

The Mental Health Act 1983 had been expected to lead to 'significant improvements' in the working of MHRTs. These clearly have not taken place. Nor have Tribunals used their increased powers to any effect. Consequently, they have done little to act as safeguard and libertarian protectors of the patients' rights. Nor has introducing High Court Judges helped matters: their presence is described by Jill Peay as 'merely symbolic'. The power of the medical profession as perceived by the Tribunal members was critical. In a revealing passage Jill Peay defines their power:

> When contradictory medical evidence was presented for example by an independent psychiatrist favouring discharge, the Tribunal would resolve its decision by arguing that this was not the best evidence. The RMO was assumed to have longstanding knowledge of the patient and would then be known to the Tribunal. In contrast the independent psychiatrist, often a stranger to the Tribunal, was assumed to reach his assessment on the basis of a 'snap-shot' view of the point. Thus evidence would be weighed accordingly, not only to its content but also its source (Peay, 1988).

Yet how is this institutional power to be attacked? How can tribunals provide the necessary safeguards? Jill Peay is for greater administrative changes. She prefers these to what she calls 're-drawing statutory criteria', which she sees as likely to have limited effectiveness. 'The quality of the safeguard depends primarily upon the abilities and inclinations of those who apply it and not on its precise wording' (Peay, 1988). Administrative changes – by which she means informal meetings between tribunal and administrative members, including the Home Office – she believes provide an invaluable forum for discussion. They help clarify mutual problems. These should result in an enhancement in the flow of information between tribunals and RMOs thereby facilitating any impact the tribunals' recommendations may have (Peay, 1988).

Whatever one may think of Jill Peay's solutions – and reading her research there is a feeling that they are rather tame compared with the fearful nature of her results – action is clearly needed. An average of one meeting every 4 months between the patients and their RMOs leads one to ask the obvious question: what do RMOs do with their time? Moreover, how is it possible to justify the enormous cost of the tribunal system when all it does is agree with the RMOs? It would have been cheaper to scrap MHRTs altogether and let the RMOs make the decision. No one doubts that the tribunal system has to make difficult decisions promoting that 'fine balance between protecting the public and the welfare of the patient which includes protecting the patient's rights'. Nor do we think the criteria easy to identify – though the Aarvold Committee set this out in an earlier report. (It thought the main considerations for MHRTs should be 'an assessment of the patient's personality, an assessment of the nature of the mental disorder, the likely response to treatment, the likelihood of a recurrence of the offence, an assessment of the situation to which the patient is [to be] released, the assessment of the patient's response to that, and an assessment of successful integration into the community or hospital (see also Bowden, 1981, p. 341).

Yet the Aarvold Committee was well aware of the problems facing MHRTs and the solution it proposed is interesting. It suggested an advisory body, independent of the treating hospital. That body would provide a second opinion. It would advise when patients displayed a risk of harm to others, or had an unfavourable and unpredictable psychiatric diagnosis. It would not override the MHRTs but assist them. One wonders if this is the answer. Statistically the categories of patients likely to produce the poorest outcome are well-known: i.e. those with an extensive criminal history, with previous admissions to psychiatric hospitals, and with a diagnosis of mental handicap or psychopathic disorder. An advisory body would draw attention to this and assist accordingly. Perhaps MHRTs would then feel more confident and challenge the medical powers if they had another body or additional data with which to do so.

The problem is not only that the MHRTs are reluctant to release patients – though that is certainly a major point to make. It is that there is nowhere for them to go. Were there better facilities outside, the Special Hospital tribunals might perhaps discharge more. That leads us back to that age-old problem of the dominance of mental hospitals and their reluctance to take the patients – with the recent added twist that mental hospitals are themselves in rapid decline.

The numbers of patients remaining in the Special Hospitals awaiting transfer remains unacceptably high. In 1989 for example 72 per cent of patients transferred had waited less than 2 years, rising to 82 per cent had waited over 3 years. But 6 per cent had waited over 6 years before being transferred (Department of Health, 1988, Special Hospital Patients Statistics HMSO, 1988). That reluctance to take the patients remains – 'a sad reflection of their unpopularity in the NHS' (Chiswick, 1982). Susanne Dell said much the same a decade or so ago. She made it clear that the 'impression often conveyed was that the everchanging string of objections was simply an attempt to make acceptable the basic and uncomfortable truth – that the hospital did not want to take patients who they feared might turn out to be difficult or even dangerous'. She added that 'the Regional and Area Health Authorities are in practice unable or unwilling to enforce hospital policies', the effect being that the decision is largely in the hands of the consultants who are unwilling to admit (Dell, 1980, p. 228). And so it remains.

Regional Secure Units

One solution was sought through the Regional Secure Units (RSUs). These are specialised purpose-built institutions, usually hospital-based providing medium security: they do not provide the levels of security of the Special Hospitals but are more secure than a locked ward of the mental hospital. They offer assessment and treatment services taking patients from the Special Hospitals, prisons, other mental hospitals, and from the courts. They were intended to solve some of the problems stated above: i.e. relieve the Special Hospitals and take offenders from the prison. They would also be expected to take patients direct from the courts, as this case record shows:

A young woman of 23 whose IQ was 65 was convicted of arson and criminal damage. Judge Verney, imposing a life sentence at Aylesbury Crown Court in October 1984 had expressed himself as very unhappy that such a woman should be sent to prison because there was no alternative available. He had cited *R*. v *Harrison* (April 13 1981) when the Court of Appeal stated that it was nothing less than a scandal that people such as the defendant in that case had to be sent to prison because there was nowhere else to send them. The convicted woman appealed. Allowing the Appeal Lord Lane the Lord Chief Justice took the opportunity to state to anyone who was prepared to listen that it was high time something was done to remedy a situation in which courts were forced to pass prison sentences on persons for whom prison was certainly not appropriate. It should be unnecessary for courts to have to keep on saying that there were people for whom a Special Hospital might not be appropriate and for whom prison was inappropriate too (quoted in *BMJ* 2 February 1985, p. 269. *R*. v. *Porter*, Court of Appeal Criminal Division, 21 January 1985)

The earliest references to the RSUs are found as far back as 1961. Initially a Ministry of Health Working Party (Ministry of Health Special Hospitals, 1961, The Emery Report) recommended that NHS hospitals should continue to provide secure out-patient provision when necessary. There was little support for the proposal – the timing was all wrong. It was the heyday of the open-door policy which swept away formal psychiatric controls in the move towards more open therapeutic environments. That led to a reconsideration of policy. The problem of the mentally abnormal offender, whether in prison or the Special Hospitals was addressed by two later Government Reports, the Glancy Report and the Butler Report (DHSS, 1973 Report on Security in NHS Hospitals, and Report of the Committee on Mentally Abnormal Offenders Cmnd 6244, 1975, The Butler Report). The Glancy Report examined the need for mentally abnormal offenders in NHS hospitals. It recognised the need for secure units for about 1000 beds in England and Wales. (Bluglass, 1978). At about the same time the Butler Committee issued an Interim Report (HMSO, Cmnd 5698, 1974) suggesting as a matter of urgency, the development of Regional Secure Units to fill the 'growing gap' provided by the overcrowded Special Hospitals and the NHS hospitals. The former provided too much security and the latter provided none at all. The Butler Committee recommended 2000 beds but the Government of the day accepted the Glancy Report's more conservative estimates of 1000 (see also Bluglass, 1978).

When the Butler Committee produced its final report in 1975 it commented on the disturbing lack of progress made in providing interim arrangements let alone more permanent ones. It thought that the difficulties which Regional Health Authorities were experiencing lay in meeting projected staff costs. In January 1976 the Government announced a special revenue allocation to each Regional Health Authority. Even then the first unit did not open until November 1980, and it took two and a half years for a further unit to open. The number of beds has been scaled down to about 800 (by 1991). By April 1985 only 120 places were available, by March 1986 this had increased to 385 (Snowden, 1986, p. 793). But even with a full complement of beds, which may not appear before the mid-1990s, the number of places are not going to make much of an impact on the overall scheme of things – if anything, they may ease some of the problems of the Special Hospitals, but would hardly scratch the surface of those from the prison.

Certainly, they have not done much so far. Yet it is not just the small number of beds that makes RSUs so ineffective when tackling the problems of the mentally abnormal offenders in prison or Special Hospitals, but the admission process and the criteria used. Admission, it seems, is on the clinical judgements of the RMOs and these are not subject to public scrutiny. Robert Bluglass sums up the position:

> Consultants jealously and justifiably retain their right to make clinical decisions based on their own judgements. If a patient cannot be offered facilities for care and treatment then the psychiatrist will indicate that he cannot be offered a bed. Technically an area medical officer (representing the manager) can direct that a patient is admitted. But the area medical officer cannot direct that a consultant takes clinical responsibility for the patient against his clinical decision and his considered judgement. Although a certain amount of pressure can be exercised eventually the attitudes of such psychiatrists and hospitals must be accepted. There is nothing to be gained by attempting to impose a policy on unwilling staff (Bluglass, 1978, p. 495).

What then are the criteria to be used for admission? No one knows. These things are not openly talked about, but Higgins (1981) speaking of one RSU offers some suggestions:

1. All patients must present a physical danger to others, and liable for detention under the compulsory powers of the Mental Health Act.

2. There must be adequate physical security on the ward to manage the patients.
3. There must be an expectation that the patient will benefit from the regime.
4. The referring medical and nursing staff must agree to take a continuing interest in their patients and agree to take them back, subject to consultation when his behaviour has improved.
5. If the patient is already in hospital it must be shown he can no longer manage in an open ward because either (a) his behaviour has very seriously threatened the physical well-being of patients or staff and is likely to be repeated or (b) if less seriously threatening, his behaviour is so repetitive and disruptive that the ward regime is completely upset.
6. A patient referred from a named central prison or special hospital must have shown recent behaviour that would prevent him from being treated in an open ward or he requires closer supervision (Higgins, 1981).

No doubt other RSUs have developed their own criteria, perhaps entirely different from the one described by Higgins. But that apart we ought not to get too excited about this impact. Admission policy is more important. In the 4 years that that particular Unit has been operating it has accepted only 39 patients, or about 10 per year: 3 from prison, 13 from remand centres and 10 from the ordinary mental hospitals. The rest come from Special Hospitals (about 1 in 2 of all referrals are admitted). On this basis it is difficult to believe that RSUs will have much impact on the problem generally – note that only about 25 per cent of all admissions were from the mental hospitals. There is little reason to suppose the RSU described by Higgins is not typical of RSUs generally. A description of the Wessex Interim Secure Unit, for example, which includes the criteria for admission, is similar (see Faulk, 1979). Clearly the RSUs take the same type of patient: acute rather than chronic, for RSUs tend to keep patients only for up to 12 months (they also jealously avoid being accused of acting as mini-Special Hospitals catering for long-term patients). They prefer short-term to long-term patients, and prefer to take those suffering from mental illness rather than the sort of patients described in the Glancy Report, i.e. the elderly wanderer, the severely mentally handicapped or the difficult patient during an acute phase of their condition (DHSS, 1974). RSUs it seems are more geared up to diagnostic activities than treatment. But who will cope with those needing long-term care? They are normally accommodated in the NHS hospitals, but with these closing down where else is there for them to go?

An assessment and some concluding thoughts

The problems for the mentally abnormal offenders are this: too many seem to be detained in prison with few opportunities for discharge or treatment. Moreover, too many remain in Special Hospitals with nowhere for them to go even though they may be suitable for less-secure conditions. The mental hospitals were once unwilling to take them. Now they are still unwilling and even if they were not there are too few hospital places anyway. RSUs take only a small number and their impact is small. Moreover RSUs do not take the long-stay chronic patient who needs the most assistance. The chronic and long-term patients seem to be out of favour with everybody.

One alternative is to develop new facilities on a larger scale. This was suggested by Bluglass (1978, p. 90) but as he says this would be expensive and unrealistic: expensive because the cost of the RSUs, are enormous with their staffing levels of about 2 staff to every 3 patients, and unrealistic because having removed the mental hospitals (to promote fiscal restraint) there would be little point building new and more expensive institutions. Another suggestion is to ensure that mental hospitals returned to the traditional role: but this too is unrealistic. As we said before, in spite of all the problems with community care we have gone too far along that road to turn back now. It must be accepted that the large mental hospitals are gone for good – and with this the mainstay of the provisions for chronic disruptive patients. Whether we like it or not these patients will have to be dealt with elsewhere, or left in the community until they commit offences, in which case they will go to the prisons until other agencies provide new forms of care.

There remains that other vexed question, the problems of the mentally disordered in the prison system. As things stand there are no adequate facilities to treat the mentally disordered within the prison system. John Gunn long ago described two forms of forensic psychiatric service – the integrated and the parallel (Gunn, 1977). Both could be used for the mentally abnormal offender. The integrated service would bring psychiatric treatment within the institutions thereby avoiding the isolation and rejection of patients by those such as the mental hospitals. This model is not likely to be accepted and Gunn believed there must be little to suggest that he should revise his thinking that unsympathetic attitudes in the NHS are likely to change sufficiently to permit such a service to function. A parallel service is all that can be hoped for, with little opportunity too transfer patients. (By 'a parallel service' Gunn meant a series of isolated institutions operating apart from others.) We already have hints of this in the way RSUs are operating. They are offering a parallel service alongside the prisons and Special Hospitals. They do not take patients from the Special Hospitals, preferring to take them direct from the courts: and they offer an acute diagnostic service rather than treatment. The prison system is also faced with the same problem. Movements towards an integrated system therefore look increasingly bleak.

The prisons it seems, need to accept the fact that they must deal with their mentally disordered patients. This conclusion seems stark yet inevitable. There will, even if goodwill exists, never be enough places outside the prison system to take everyone. As Faulk says 'should a state of affairs ever be reached in which the NHS and Social Services have the facilities to accept from the penal system all the cases which medical men will agree upon, the penal systems would still find that they had in their care many severely disordered people' (Faulk, 1979). There is certainly a lack of goodwill at present. One reason, as the Royal College of Psychiatrists say, the open-door policy where 'many people, enlisting doctors and nurses working in psychiatric hospitals have been concerned that the admissions of significant numbers of mentally abnormal offenders will reverse the trend' (*BMJ*, 29 November 1980, p. 1446). Another is thought to be that psychiatry is only concerned with high technical medicine and short-stay patients: prisoners do not fit into those categories.

The predictions of Dr Peter Scott seem to have been realised. He believed that RSUs would become increasingly selective: they would follow the rules set by the mental hospitals and not accept the more difficult patients who present the main problem to the psychiatric services (Scott, 1970). His solution was to suggest that the prisons should deal with their own mentally abnormal offenders. In this we must agree.

Rather than endeavouring to lift the mentally abnormal out of prison into hospital (where experience suggests they are not welcome) it might be better to acknowledge that there are certain varieties of mentally abnormal persons . . . who are much better treated in prison. This could have the great advantage that . . . treatment facilities . . . would be available for the whole prison system. This would be the exact reversal of the Mental Health Act principle of removing patients to be treated and of the implication that what remains needs none. It is already a fact that the medical complement of certain prison establishments is proportionately much greater than in many mental hospitals and it is likely that in future prisons and mental hospitals will increasingly overlap (Scott, in *BMJ*, 18 April 1975, p. 168).

Scott has been wrong in one respect: prison and mental hospitals have not overlapped. Prisons have become more sophisticated and there are fewer mental hospitals. But much else in his predictions has come about. We agree that the mentally abnormal offenders will have to be treated in prison and where there is experience in the ways to deal with them, especially the severe ones – severe in the sense of the type of offence committed rather than of the mental disorder.

Scott's views will not please everyone. The prison is seen by many as an inappropriate place to treat the mentally disordered, or they say adequate facilities are not yet available. Still others say that the presence of adequate facilities for treatment may actually encourage courts to send more people to prison: that being the only place where in-patient treatment is available. The latter objection must be given serious consideration. Already there is a mistaken belief that treatment is available in prison. Judges are occasionally heard to say, 'I'm sending you to prison where you will receive psychiatric treatment.' One can see how they might find prison an easier and more justifiable sentencing option if they were persuaded that treatment could be given. If the prison psychiatric services are to be increased more restrictions must be placed on the courts' powers of sentencing.

There remain other problems with the Special Hospitals. Neither the Butler Committee nor any other authoritative group has advocated doing away with the Special Hospitals – though some voices are beginning to be heard advancing such ideas. The Royal College of Psychiatrists concluded that Special Hospitals were necessary and would continue to exist in the foreseeable future. But the problem remains how to get patients out. Transfers can take place between the Special Hospitals and the State Mental Hospitals. Also under section 123(2) of the Mental Health Act 1983 the Secretary of State is empowered to direct the transfer of a Special Hospital patient to an NHS hospital. We are not however aware of any such order being made so far (up to and including 1991, that is). But current policies are moving towards putting financial pressures on mental hospitals to pay the cost of keeping patients in Special Hospitals whilst they are awaiting transfer, although this does not solve the problem of lack of facilities to take them. The solution is bound to be difficult and long-term: the hoped-for solution that the MHRTs would help to get patients out of the Special Hospitals has clearly not worked, yet MHRTs offer remains the best, and possibly the only, hope.

Changes in the manner is which tribunals operate will certainly help but unless the RSUs have the facilities to take more transferred patients and can be persuaded to do so, these changes will be thwarted. Perhaps the only real solution is to continue in the direction that we are going, putting fewer patients in the Special Hospitals. When it becomes difficult to get them out, the Secretary of State should use his powers to do so. But who will provide the finance to increase the places to take them? The Royal College of Psychiatrists is right in one sense: the problem which has been described in the national press as a scandal, i.e. that 10 per cent of Special Hospital patients remain in conditions of maximum security long after they need do so, still requires urgent attention (Royal College of Psychiatrists, 1983, *The Future of the Special Hospitals*). That is the other problem of discharges.

8
Conclusion

The process of dismantling the mental hospital system has proceeded at such a pace that considerations about rationalising it,
have been left behind by events. Sending patients out of the
mental hospitals has been a main feature of central Government
policy for nearly thirty years, but has more recently gathered
momentum. What we know about this process is limited: what
we think we know is a great deal. What we can expect to happen
is anybody's guess, hence our attempt in this book to map out
some of the likely contours.

What seems reasonably clear however is that decarceration has
not led to a drastic decline in admissions. Quite the opposite. It
has created a new 'revolving door' effect, where fewer patients
are admitted initially, but are returning for more admissions,
perhaps because they do not stay long enough in hospital to
recover fully. This phenomenon seems more marked where community psychiatry has been operating the longest.

Deinstitutionalisation is a social ideology which means that
now everyone (with the exception of some categories of mentally
abnormal offenders) gets out of hospitals, although the plight of
some groups of patients after leaving may be quite different. And
the concept of 'discharge' itself is not necessarily as simplistic as
to mean 'leaving hospital', like it once was. For a lot of people a
short stay in hospital can mean the beginning of months, or years
or even a lifetime of contact with psychiatric services in the community. This is an area about which we know very little and
which would repay a good deal more careful study. How does
one escape from out-patient community psychiatry? Does it or
can it ever end? We remain doubtful for there are no longer clear
distinctions between the stages within the system, out-patient
blurs with in-patient and out-patient with 'freedom' where the
possibility of being recalled into the psychiatric fold must always
remain.

The second factor about which we can be reasonably clear is that provision of care in the community has not progressed as fast as the move to release patients. The organisation of statutory and voluntary agencies to cope with these has been slow. At the same time central government policies have worked against the organisation of community care, with the introduction of the new benefit system (which discriminates against more than half of the long-stay patients leaving hospital, as shown in Chapter 2), works together with the housing situation (which now caters for families rather than single people) to make it impossible for patients to settle and survive in the community.

The function of mental hospitals to provide asylum or sanctuary to those people who could not and never would survive in the community, has been ignored in favour of a more treatment-orientated community-care philosophy. The growth in numbers of private nursing homes provides this function (of asylum) for those patients over retirement age, but as we say earlier this is not deinstitutionalisation, but 'transinstitutionalisation', where one institution is exchanged for another. In no way could these psychiatric patients be considered to live independently, have responsibility for their own lives or be said to be a part of the community.

It is often said that we can tell a lot about a society by the way it treats its elderly. In Western European societies we have an aging society (the members in the over-75-years-old group have increased 30 per cent since 1976 in Britain) which is expected to become increasingly so. The growth in the number of private nursing homes tells us a lot about the perception of old age. Responsibility, it seems, has passed from the family to the private sector, where it is now big business and profitable to commit the elderly to an institution, albeit in the 'Community'. For long-stay elderly patients getting out of hospital can mean just as disabling, or frightening or dehumanising a life as the formally structured mental institutions were. We have met few elderly persons in either private or state care who preferred that type of institutional life to their own homes however. The pervading emotion seems to be depression explained not by the usual psychiatric aetiologies, but by the position in which they find themselves. And worst of all, we call it progress, or more precisely 'reform'.

Unhappily the fate of patients leaving hospital will be different for every group and we have identified these in Chapter 4. This variability in after-care, we feel, should not happen if each patient left hospital only after a careful, individual, planning procedure. But there is no evidence to suggest that any such planning occurs, at least on a large enough scale. Rehabilitation programmes were and are supposed to be the answer; preparing patients for the community is expensive and placing patients in the community following such programmes is jeopardised by both the housing situation and the benefit system, as mentioned before. Numbers, therefore, remain small compared with the overall numbers of discharged patients leaving each year. This has led the Government, the Royal College of Psychiatrists and the Mental Health Act Commission alike to issue the first guidelines on discharge and after-care procedures to prepare the way in the 1990s – some 30 years after the idea of closure of mental hospitals was first muted. We wonder why we had to wait so long?

Rehabilitation itself – the ideology and the practice – has been with us a long time. Yet little or no resources have been allocated to it; certainly no monies are forthcoming from the sale of land after the closure of large hospitals. Rehabilitation with all its models and approaches remains the only hope which the current hospital population has, to make a successful transition from institutions to community, for it is the only programme that attempts to individualise the personal needs of each patient. However, the staff who operate such programmes are often those who have worked in the old-style institutions and are not always totally equipped themselves to function as therapists outside the hospital in a therapeutic milieu of which they have little experience. For as Paul Sayer asked in *The Comforts of Madness*:

> Where did they find the initiative, this animated desire to take me apart, build me up, re-invent me? I had no satisfactory answer, save the recurrent notion that somehow they were really attempting a reconstruction of their own selves, imposing on me an image of the way they thought they were, or should be (Sayer, 1988).

The reality of preparing someone for a community existence is dependent on a subjective judgement of one person's view of the community which may very well be different from that of another. But who is to say which 'reality' is correct? Our successes and failures will depend upon who will 'fit in' and who will not, as well as the appropriateness of the programme to achieve this.

The new community programmes and ways of working seem destined to follow the same course as experienced in the USA. Moreover, it is far from certain whether the care they offer will actually reach those people who need it most. We feel sure it will not. The tendency, it seems, is to neglect the patients with long-term serious mental illness in favour of those with less-severe problems, i.e. emotional or situational disturbances, those we call the 'worried well'. The evidence emerging in Britain already suggests this is so.

The idea of provision in the community would, it was argued, allow accessibility because services would be housed in ordinary buildings in the high street. This aim was short-lived, however, as concentrations of such resources in certain neighbourhoods made accessibility more difficult (at least for those who needed them most) than hospital-based services which already lay on public transport routes.

Furthermore, we are worried about the increasing groups of people kicked up by the new services and who had hitherto not used them. By operating in the community, psychiatrists no longer have to wait for the severely disturbed to be referred to the mental hospital; being available in General Practice surgeries and in their newly acquired sector-bases, their expertise is sought for all cases of recognisable mental illness. Perhaps GPs themselves could learn from the 'expert' psychiatrist how to recognise mental illness more easily and thus refer a second opinion. The police, with their experience of severely disturbed people in public places have proved to be expert at recognising psychiatric illness, the position in the future is that they will be more likely than hitherto to encounter serious mental illness like psychosis.

Certainly, the provision of community services has been much slower than has been the closure of hospitals. It is true to say that leaving hospital is the beginning of many problems for a lot of patients. Life can be hard, lonely and distressing for those who are exchanging a good institution for a bad experience in a hostile community. The traditional functions of the mental hospital have not been totally replicated in the community. Treatment has, but asylum (seen as 'sanctuary' – a place of safety) has not. If community care was driven by a concern to eradicate that which was inherently bad about institutional life it has not always been successful.

The intention behind the destruction of the hospital system was the abolition of the harsh and coercive elements that had reinforced and sustained its dominance for nearly two centuries. But has it been fulfilled? We think not. The use of coercion to keep patients in institutions was expected to disappear if the system itself were removed. In Chapter 4 we have shown that this is not necessarily what happens in practice. The use of the Mental Health Act 1983 could have been expected to decline proportionately with the decrease in the numbers of patients going into institutions. This has apparently been foiled both by the increase in readmission rates in the new system and the tendency to want to use the Act as if it related to the community – or rather to see the community as an extension of the mental hospital.

Moreover, some would see this tendency as an indication that there is a need for a Community Treatment Order, which would extend coercion into the community thus making the community the central arena for treatment and the hospital the 'back-up' facility. This we do not consider to be either progress, or in the best interests of the patient. It is for these reasons that we maintain that the concept of 'discharge' has changed. 'Discharge' no longer means leaving the hospital: it now means that the discontinuation of contact with psychiatric services, which usually occurs in the community, if at all. Whether or not it occurs depends on the type of patient discharged. The elderly patient with organic conditions can be said to be 'discharged' from hospital to a community-based institution e.g. Part III accommodation or private nursing home, and they will have no further contact. Others like the younger schizophrenics or manic depressives who return home or to private residences will have the most contact with psychiatric services, if they can. Those going through the rehabilitation route will never be 'discharged', but will remain on someone's books indefinitely.

The care that they will receive in the community will be organised in a variety of ways. One of these ways we have described in Chapter 4 and is called sectorisation. This is the administrative means by which community psychiatry has been organised in some areas or districts in this country. Have these new ways of organisation reduced the need for social controls within the mental hospitals? Again we think not, for we fear the current temptation is to utilise and adapt these to suit the new community ways of working. Instead of declining with the decreasing hospital population, formal detention has increased, as has the practice of releasing detained patients allowing their sections to expire in the community.

Some people would argue that such practices demonstrate a clear need for the proposed Community Treatment Order (CTO) which would enable patients to be compulsorily treated in their own homes. But as we have shown in Chapter 5, these proposals are unduly optimistic about their effectiveness and ignore the differences between the hospital setting and that of the community. The mental hospital had represented a restrictive and coercive form of social control for over two centuries and critics condemned it for its harshness and inhumanity. The CTO, we think, is no more humane and no less harsh, for we can not believe that it in any way benefits the mentally ill to be forcibly treated in their own homes (even if this were possible).

With the changes in the structure of mental health care there should have emerged consideration of the rights of mental patients in the community. Yet these have been largely overlooked. For too long mental patients have been seen as not responsible for their actions and consequently they have forfeited rights until they resume full health again. In Chapter 6 we have argued that as a social group, they hold little political power and are seldom taken seriously; their demands go unheard and they do not have the power to make themselves heard, as others usually act for them. The 1983 Act makes this clear in the fact that consent to treatment does not give them the right to refuse treatment (or indeed to demand it where none is forthcoming); it merely gives patients a second medical opinion which allows treatment to be enforced.

We have examined the powerfulness of the law to explore rights – where they exist – but we are hard-pushed to find laws that confer rights. We have examined the difference between legal rights and moral rights, and using a positivist theory of rights we find that there is no right where there is no power to secure the object of the right. Moral rights are not legal rights unless they have been established by law. Unless mental patients have the right to refuse treatment (rather than just to consent to it) they have no rights in relation to treatment.

Moreover, in matters of rights in relation to malpractice, psychiatrists are seemingly less likely than are other medical practitioners to suffer claims against them, although this is gradually changing. Litigation is increasing also where patients discharged to the community injure a third party. We think the practice and the debate will continue as more hospitals close and little attention is paid to rights in general in respect of patients being treated in the community. Especially do we think that litigation will be helped by the practice of psychiatry itself. Psychiatry, we have said, has no central orthodoxy, no agreed standards of care or procedures for undertaking treatment. This eventually will also apply to the multidisciplinary staff.

Above all else there are no rights for mental patients to be let out of hospitals in England and Wales, as there are elsewhere. There are elaborate rules relating to admissions, but none about leaving. Neither do patients have any right *not* to leave if they are not ready. The decision to send patients out remains the sole province of clinicians, as Jill Peay has shown. Mental Health Review Tribunals tend only to reinforce clinical decisions. If this is so then mentally abnormal offenders in Special Hospitals have special problems, for if mental hospitals close down their chances of discharge become remote. They may have become marooned and remain there longer than they need to, as is already happening.

Treatment has been transferred to the community, but the traditional function of custodial care has not – for how could it be? There will always be the need to protect some people from themselves and society from others. Special hospitals and prisons have come more and more to take on this role. But how will people ever find themselves able to get out of these places if the community has no halfway facility to take them now that the mental hospital is a thing of the past?

One major structural change brought about by these 'reforms' has been in the role of psychiatry itself, but more specifically in that of psychiatrists. We have argued strongly, here and elsewhere, that the structural position of psychiatry has strengthened. Psychiatrists have exchanged their traditional power-base in mental hospitals to expand into general hospitals alongside the physicians and the surgeons, as well as out into the community to encroach on the GPs' domain, presenting themselves as 'experts' in the care of the mentally ill.

They have expanded to present the world with an entourage – the multidisciplinary team, consisting of social workers, nurses, psychologists, behavioural therapists and occupational therapists. And these auxiliary staff now emulate the medical approach and in so doing reinforce the credibility of the *power* of psychiatry. And we think it sad, if this is the only achievement in the case of mental illness, for it was William Beveridge (with high hopes for our Welfare State) as long ago as 1953 who warned us:

> Power as a means of getting things done appeals to that which men share with brutes, to fear and to greed; power leads those who wield it to desire it for its own sake, not for the service it may render, and to

seek its continuance in their own hands. Influence as a means of getting things done appeals to that which distinguishes men from brutes. The way out of the world's troubles today is to treat men as men, to enthrone influence over power, and to make power revocable (Beveridge, 1953).

To repeat a point made earlier, we have moved too far along the road of decarceration, and indeed sectorisation to go back now. The old-style mental hospital, whether we like it or not, has gone for good and the new-style form of community care has taken over. That model of psychiatric care will remain with us for the next generation at least, forcing other pieces of the mental health jigsaw to be replaced, reshaped and relocated. The mental patient who is mad and bad, i.e. the mentally disordered offender, will probably be affected as much as any but so too will be the new chronic – the elderly demented.

If we may make national generalisations from the situation in Nottingham, our data show some of the shortfalls of the present system: that sectorisation may actually produce an increase in compulsory orders is an alarming thought, and that the number (and presumably quality) of post-release contacts is so small shows how few people leaving hospital are provided with a continuum of care. It is too easy to see the solution in financial terms – i.e. that more money should be spent on community programmes. If the closure of mental hospitals was brought about by the Government's desire to save money – and it is reasonable to suppose this to be true – it would seem foolish to expect Governments to increase spending in the community up to the levels of earlier spending in the hospital. That would defeat the whole purpose of the exercise.

What then to do? The first thing is to find out more about what is going on and treat claims that community care is the solution to all mental health problems with much scepticism. Never was there a time when more information was required, and never a time when enthusiasm for a new ideology (community care) should be more closely examined. Such a careful examination is necessary and should be regarded as more important than any ideologies. Mental health systems have suffered a surfeit of ideologies in the past 25 years and the time has come to take stock of what there is, and what is happening. We doubt if there is a more urgent need for data than now.

The second thing to do is to clarify where the responsibility lies and who is responsible for making the decisions. To be told that the patient is to be treated by a 'community care team' makes it difficult for anyone, least of all the patient, to know who is responsible for that treatment. The possibility always exists of officials hiding behind a collective decision or avoiding taking decisions altogether. It is not just the community team who operate in this way, the problem pervades the whole of the mental health service and indeed the so-called caring professions generally. The whole process begins a long way back as far as mental patients are concerned: it begins with the legislation requiring two doctors to make the medical recommendations (why not one? why continue with the fiction that two doctors will act as a corrective to each other when it is clear that the psychiatrist *de facto* makes the decision?) and continues now into community treatment programmes. That type of collective responsibility may be comforting to the community team but we doubt if it gives comfort or inspires confidence in anyone else, least of all the patients. It certainly protects, and will doubtless continue to protect members of the community team from litigation where negligence is alleged – that we are clear about.

The third thing to do is to avoid being stampeded into new control systems such as the Community Treatment Order, which as we have argued is an ill considered attempt to transfer the whole of the hospital to the community. As we keep saying, the community is not a watered-down mental hospital, or a more open yet therapeutic version of a closed institution. The norms and values differ, as do the goals and roles of its numbers. The danger of being stampeded into a decision which seems, on the face of it, quite reasonable is very real. What is also certain is that the demands will not end then. Another group of patients will be identified, also said to need special provisions (read 'control' for 'provisions') and before we know where we are new legislation is implemented and off we go again. The American position is instructive here: they have a CTO in some states: that has led to preventive commitment orders. Now pregnant women who are drug-users have been identified as a group at risk and provisions exists to detain them until their children are born. Other drug-users can be compulsorily detained for being drug-users. And so it goes on. It is our firm belief that the solutions to such problems, mental health or drug abuse are not to be found in new and more demanding control systems. More likely they are found in good practice.

Fourthly we think there is a need to monitor more carefully the types of care provided by the process of 'transinstitutionalisation' whether they be privately supplied or not. Too often there are reports of restraints being used on elderly patients, being tied to the chair or being provided with medication which has the same overall effect. These controls are as invidious as anything used in the mental hospitals. We suspect that where such controls are used they have less to do with staffing ratios (it is easy to blame shortage of staff for every defect) more to do with the quality of the regime. Our hypothesis is that homes or institutions which attempt to stimulate patients will require fewer controls. Leaving patients in their isolated depressed worlds, forcing them into a form of communal living, or expecting the television to act as a magical instrument of stimulation or as a way of passing the time we do not think is the answer.

Finally we think new legislation is beginning to be required to take account of some of the changes we have tried to document here. The Mental Health Act Commission in England and Wales, for example, was a response to conditions in the late 1970s not to the those of the 1990s. Its remit was to be concerned only with compulsory patients. This was most admirable given the position of patients in the mental hospitals (and relevant nowadays given the recent increase in compulsory admissions) but this is only part of the problem. There are no powers for the Commission to deal with those elderly patients in old people's homes described above, who are rarely on a compulsory order but whose detention is no less real than any on a compulsory order in hospital. And what of new legislation to clarify some of the rights and expectations which patients might now have? Why not think of new methods to deal with compulsory admissions? We are still not sure what a social worker or nearest relation is expected to do in the compulsory admission procedure for, as we have asked earlier, why is there a need for two doctors to make the medical recommendation? A clarification of the powers of the community team is now overdue.

New legislation is of course for the future, and mental health acts tend to come only about every 25 years. But as we are nearly 10 years from the last one we should be thinking of the next one soon.

Notes

Chapter 4

1. We are grateful to the Editors of the *Journal of Law Medicine and Health Care* for permission to reproduce some of the material here.

Chapter 5

1. The circumstances of the cases are these (and they have been spelled out rather fully to reflect the importance of the case. This information is taken from the Law Report, Queen's Bench Division 1986, pp. 1109).

   In its judgement the High Court concentrated on three Sections of the Mental Health Act 1983 Section 3 of the 1983 Act concerned with admission to hospital and detention, which says 'A person admitted to hospital becomes an in-patient, and the admission is for treatment.' Section 3(1) says 'A patient may be admitted to a hospital and detained there for the period allowed by the . . . provision of this Act . . . ' Section 17 says 'The responsible medical officer may grant to any patient who is for the time being liable to the detained in a hospital . . . leave to be absent subject to such considerations (if any) as that officer considers necessary in the interests of the patient or for the protection of other persons. Leave of absence may be granted to a patient under this section either indefinitely or for a specified period. However, a patient to whom leave of absence is granted shall not be recalled after he has ceased to be liable to be detained.' This Section goes on to say 'and any such patients shall cease to be liable at the expiration of the period of 6 months beginning with the first day of his absence unless he has returned to the hospital'.

   Finally, Section 20 says: 'Subject to the following provision of the Act a patient admitted to hospital in pursuance of an application for admission to treatment may be detained in a hospital . . . for a period not exceeding 6 months beginning with the day on which he was so admitted . . . but shall not be so detained . . . for any longer unless the authority for his detention is renewed under the Section.' These sections were taken together in the High Court.

   The applicants *W* and *L* had been admitted to hospital on many previous occasions for treatment for their mental disorders. *W* was living in a hostel but refusing to take her medication. It was considered by the appropriate medical authorities that she should be admitted to hospital for treatment under Section 3 of the 1983 Act. W was admitted for 1 night and thereafter granted leave of absence under Section 17. In the belief that W was 'liable to be detained' provisions relating to current treatment no longer applied.

L who had been detained for treatment under Section 3 (1984) was granted leave of absence under Section 17 two months later. He went to live at home. His responsible medical officer considered it was essential for him to continue to take medication while remaining at home but he was refusing to accept it. Three months later (May 1985) his responsible medical officer, purporting to act under Section 17, reported that it was necessary for L's health for him to receive treatment which could not be provided when he was detained, and in consequence they purported to renew the authority for his liability to be detained which had been due to expire on 17 June, i.e. 6 months after being first detained. L remained at home. Subsequently the medical officer (Dr Gardner) mistakenly believing that his ability to be detained was due to expire on 26 September (it being 6 months since L last visited the hospital), wrote on 23 September 1985 telling him to return to hospital with the intention of intercepting his leave before the expiry of the 6-month period. L did not return to hospital.

In W's case, the Queen's Bench Division held that Section 3 of the Act creates jurisdiction to admit a patient to hospital for treatment compulsorily. The section clearly meant and was intended to mean that the patient should be admitted with in-patient status (the Act says 'may be admitted to a hospital and detained there' and 'appropriate for him to receive medical treatment in a hospital'). Oliver Thorold representing W held that grounds for admission cannot be made out if doctors supplying the necessary recommendation do not believe that a period of in-patient treatment is required. In L's case there are two parts to the judicial decision. First on the question of the justification for renewal of authority to detain a patient under Section 20: this, said the court, only arose when the doctor believed that the mental condition of the patient necessitated a further period of detention for treatment as an in-patient. In L's case the decision to send the letter of recall was not based on any clinical judgements. The timing of the letter appears to have been based on nothing more than a calendar calculation that 6 months from L's visit to the hospital (on 26 March 1985) was about to relapse. But, to complicate matters further, that recall letter had no effect because L had already been on leave of absence for longer than 6 months. His visit to the hospital on 26 March to see a Doctor Carr would not, said the Court, render L a patient. L visited solely to deal with matters relating to consent to treatment.

On the second matter the Court held that it was unlawful to recall to hospital a patient on indefinite leave of absence when the intention was merely to prevent him from being on leave of absence for 6 months continuously. Section 17(4) only empowered the responsible medical officer to revoke the leave of absence and recall the patient when it was necessary for the patient's health or safety or for the protection of other persons, and therefore the purported recall – the letter of 23 September – would have been unlawful even if he had been liable to be detained after 17 June. And in an important passage the following points were made:

(a) Once a patient has been on leave of absence for 6 months his liability to be recalled ends (Section 17 (5)). To frustrate the provision of the device of recall for one night, for which recall there is no necessity, is to extend the duration of the liability to recall. Express provision for the extension of such liability has been made under Section 20. To use Section 17 (6) in the way under consideration is to by-pass the requirements of Section 20.

(b) There can only be two intentions behind the device. One is to extend the period during which a patient may be treated compulsorily in the community. The other is to retain the power to recall him should consideration of his health or safety or the protection of others require this at some time in the future. In neither event could it truly be said that 'it is necessary so to do'. (i.e. to detain compulsorily as an in-patient "in the interests of (his) health or safety or for the protection of the other persons".

The court's decision closed off the so-called 'long-leash' arrangements, or put differently Section 17 of the 1983 Mental Health Act could no longer be lawfully used to produce the effect of a long-term community treatment order.

2. The proposal to insert a clause in the Disabled Persons (Services Consultation Representation) Bill was more a gesture than of serious intent. The Registrar of the Royal College of Psychiatrists (Professor RG Priest) sent a letter to Tom Clarke, MP, on 26 February 1986, asking if he would table an amendment to the Bill which under Clause 4 would allow the introduction of a community treatment order. Professor Priest argued that the Bill under that clause dealt with the provision of services for psychiatric patients when they leave hospital and the Royal College of Psychiatrists believed that their amendment would clarify the law on the medical treatment of such patients in the community. Mr Clarke did not move the amendment. Another attempt by the Royal College occurred when Dr

Gordon Langley, a psychiatrist, wrote to Mr John Hannam, MP, another sponsor of the Bill, asking if amendments could be made for Clause 4 of the Bill to provide compulsory treatment for the mentally ill for whom less restrictive options had failed. This too was put out – the reasons for which have not been made public.

Bibliography

Allderidge, P. (1979) 'Hospitals, Madhouses and Asylums: Cycles in the Care of the Insane', *British Journal of Psychiatry*, vol. 134, pp. 321–34.

Allen, F. A. (1959) 'Criminal Justice, Legal Values and the Rehabilitative Ideal', *Journal of Criminal Law, Criminology and Police Science*, vol. 50, pp. 226–32.

American Correctional Association (1972) 'Developments of Modern Concepts and Standards', in Carter, R. M., Glaser, D. and Williams, L. T. (eds), *Correctional Institutions*' (New York: Lippincott).

American Psychiatric Association (1987) *Involuntary Commitment to Outpatient Treatment*, Task Force Report no. 26.

Arlidge, J. T. (1859) *On the State of Lunacy and the Legal Provision for the Insane* (Edinburgh: Churchill).

Armstrong, D. (1980) 'Madness and Coping', *Sociology of Health and Illness*, vol. 2, pp. 293–316.

Audit Commission Study (1987) *Community Care: Developing Services for People with Mental Handicap*, Occasional Paper 4 (London: HMSO).

Bachrach, L. (1976) *Deinstitutionalisation: An Analytical Review and Sociology Perspective*, National Institute of Mental Health Series D, no. 4 (Washington: US Dept of Health, Education and Welfare).

Barnett, C. R. (1975) 'An Anthropologist's Perspective', in Howard, J. and Strauss, A. (eds), *Humanising Health Care* (New York: Wiley).

Barton, R. (1959) *Institutional Neurosis* (Bristol: Wright).

Bassuk, E. L. and Gerson, S. (1978) 'Deinstitutionalisation and Mental Health Services', *Scientific American*, 238, pp. 46–53.

Bates, P. and Walsh, M. (1989): *Empty Premises – Empty Promises*, Benefits Research Unit Occasional Paper 1/89, Nottingham.

Bean, P. T. (1976) *Rehabilitation and Deviance* (London: Routledge & Kegan Paul).

Bean, P. T. (1980) *Compulsory Admissions to Mental Hospitals* (New York: Wiley).

Bean, P. T. (1986) *Mental Disorder and Legal Control* (Cambridge University Press).

Bean, P. T. (1988) 'Mental Health Care in Europe: Some Recent Trends', in Smith, C. J. and Giggs, J. A. (eds), *Location and Stigma: Contemporary Perspectives in Mental Health and Mental Health Care* (London: Unwin Hyman).

Bean, P. T. and Mounser, P. (1989) 'Community Care and the Discharge of Patients from Mental Hospitals', *American Journal of Law, Medicine and Health Care*, vol. 17, no. 2, February.

Bean P. T. *et al.* (1991) *Out of Harm's way* (London: MIND).

Becker, S., Hannan, J. and Hyde, S. (1988) *Guide to the Social Fund Manual* (Nottingham: Benefits Research Unit).

Becker, A. and Schulberg, H. D. (1976) 'Phasing Out State Hospitals – a Psychiatric Dilemma', *New England Journal of Medicine*, 294; pp. 255–61.

Benn, S. I. and Peter, R. S. (1975) *Social Principles and the Democratic State* (London: Allen & Unwin).

Bennett D. (1983) *Rehabilitation: The Way Ahead or the End of the Road*, in Herbert, KS (ed) (London: The Mental Health Foundation).

Berger, P. and Luckmann, T. (1967) *The Social Construction of Reality* (London: Allen Lane).

Berry, G. and Orwin, A. (1986) 'No Fixed Abode', *British Journal of Psychiatry*, 112, pp. 1029–25.

Beveridge, W. (1953) *Power and Influence* (London: Hodder & Stoughten).

Bingley, W. (1985) 'Mental Health Legislation in England and Wales, in Jenson, K. and Pendersen, B. (eds), *Commitment and Civil Rights of the Mentally Ill* (SIN Cophenhagen).

Bluglass, R. (1978) 'Regional Secure Units and Interim Security for Psychiatric Patient's', *British Medical Journal*, (25 February) pp. 489–93.

Boardman, A. P. (ed.) (1988) *Community Mental Health Centres in the United Kingdom – The Example of the Mental Health Advice Centre in Lewisham* (London: NUPRD).

Boardman, A. P., Bouras, N. and Cundy, J. (1986) 'Evaluation of a Community Mental Health Centre', *Acta Psychiatrica* (Beig), pp. 402–6.

Boardman, A. P., Bouras, N. and Cundy, J. (1987) *The Mental Health Advice Centre in Lewisham. Service Usage: trends from 1978–1984* (London: NUPRD).

Bowden, P. (1981) 'What Happens to Patients Released from Special Hospitals', *British Journal of Psychiatry*, vol. 138, pp. 340–5.

Brazier, M. (1987) *Medicine, Patients and the Law* (Harmondsworth: Penguin).

British Association of Social Workers (1977) *Mental Health Crisis Services: A New Philosophy* (London: BASW).

British Medical Journal, 29 November 1980, p. 1446.

British Medical Journal, 2 February 1985, p. 269.

British Medical Journal, 9 February 1985, vol. 290, p. 447.

Bromley, E. (1989) 'Compulsory Treatment in the Community; An Alternative View, mimeo.

Brook, A. (1978) 'An Aspect of Community Mental Health: Consultative Work with General Practice Teams', *Health Trends*, 2, pp. 37–9.

Brook, P. and Cooper, B. (1975) 'Community Mental Health Care: Primary Team Specialist Services', *Journal of the Royal College of General Practitioners*, 25, pp. 93–110.

Brough, D. I., Bouras, N. and Watson, P. (1988) 'The Mental Health Advice Centre in Lewisham', in Boardman, A. P. (ed.), *Community Mental Health Centres in the United Kingdom – The Example of the Mental Health Advice Centre in Lewisham* (London: NUPRD).

Brough, D. I. and Watson, J. P. (1977) 'Psychiatric Facilities in an "Over-Resourced" NHS region', *British Medical Journal*, 1 October 1977.

Brown, P. (1985) *The Transfer of Care: Psychiatric Deinstitutionalisation and Its Aftermath* (New York: Routledge).

Burke, G. (1981) *Housing and Social Justice: The Role of Policy in British Housing.* Longman: London.

Busfield, J. (1986) *Managing Madness: Changing Ideas and Practice* (London: Hutchinson).

Campbell, T. (1988) *Justice* (London: Macmillan).

Chiswick, D. (1982) 'The Special Hospitals: A Problem of Clinical Credibility', *Bulletin of the Royal College of Psychiatrists'*, vol. 16, pp. 13–132.

Clare, A. (1980) *Psychiatry in Dissent*, 2nd edn (London: Tavistock).

Clare, A. W. and Shepherd, M. (1978) 'Psychiatry and Family Medicine', in Fry, J., Gambrill, E. and Smith, R. (eds) *Scientific Foundations of Family Medicine* (London: Heinemann) pp. 105–23.

Cloward, R. A. (1960) 'Social Control in the Prisons', *Studies in the Social Organisation of the Prison* (New York: Research Council in Social Science).

Cohen, D. (1988) *Forgotten Millions: The Treatment of the Mentally Ill – a Global Perspective* (London: Paladin Grafton).

Coid, J. (1984) 'How Many Psychiatric Patients in Prison', *British Journal of Psychiatry*, vol. 145, pp. 78–86.

Connolly, J. (1830) *An Inquiry Concerning the Indications of Insanity* (London:).

Cooper, B., Harwin, B. G., Bepla, C. and Shepherd, M. (1975) 'Mental Health Care in the Community: An Evaluative Study', *Psychological Medicine*, 5, pp. 372–80.

Corney, R. H. and Briscoe, M. E. (1977) 'Social Workers and their Clients: A Comparison between Primary Health Care and Local Authority Settings', *Journal of the Royal College of General Practitioners*, 27, pp. 295–307.

Corser, C. M. and Ryce, S. W. (1977) 'Community Mental Health Care: A Model Based on the Primary Care Team', *British Medical Journal*, ii, pp. 936–8.

Davis, N. and Tutt, A. (1983) 'The Mental Health Act 1983 – Greater Workload for Medical Records Officers?' Nottingham Psychiatric Case Register, in mimeo.

Delman, J. (1980) 'Alternatives to Hospitalization: Advocacy Now', *Journal of Patients' Rights and Mental Health Advocacy*, September 1980, vol. 2, no. 3.

Dell, S. (1980) The Transfer of Special Hospital Patients to the NHS Hospitals. Special Hospitals Research Unit Report Unit No. 16.

DHSS (1974) 'Revised Report of the Working Party on Security in NHS Psychiatric Hospitals' (unpublished) The Glancy Report.

DHSS (1975) *Better Services for the Mentally Ill*, Cmnd 6233 (London: HMSO).

DHSS (1983) *Mental Health Act 1983 – Memorandum on Parts I to VI, VIII and X* (London: Dept of Health and Social Security).

DHSS (1989) Press Release (13 July).

DHSS (1990) 'Health Services Development: Caring for People – The Care Programme Approach for People with Mental Illness', draft paper.

Durham, M. and La Fond, J. (1988) 'A Search for the Missing Premise of Involuntary Therapeutic Commitment: Effective Treatment of the Mentally Ill', *Rutgers Law Review*, vol. 40, no. 2.

Edwalds, R. M. (1964) 'Functions of the State Mental Hospital as a Social Institution', *Mental Hygiene*, 48; pp. 666–71.

Faulk, M. (1979) 'Mentally Disordered Offenders in an Interim Regional Secure Unit', *Criminal Law Review*, pp. 686–95.

Faulkner, L. R., Terwilliger, W. B. and Cutler, D. L. (1984) 'Productive Activities for the Chronic Patient', *Community Mental Health Journal*, Summer, vol. 20, no. 2, pp. 110–11.

Fennell, P. (1986) 'Law and Psychiatry: The Legal Constitution of the Psychiatric System', *Journal of Law and Society*, vol. 13, pp. 35–65.

Furlong, R. C. S., Brough, D. I. and Watson, J. P. (1988) *Lewisham Mental Health Advice Centre: A New Development in Community Care* (London: NUPRD).

GLC Health Panel (1984) *Mental Health Services in London*.

Goffman, E. (1961) *Asylums* (New York: Doubleday, reprinted 1997 by Penguin Books, Harmondsworth).

Goldberg, D. and Huxley, P. (1980) *Mental Illness in the Community: The Pathway to Psychiatric Care* (London: Tavistock).

Goldie, N. (1977) 'The Division of Labour among the Mental Health Professionals – a Negotiated or Imposed Order?' in Stacey *et al.* (ed.), *Health and the Division of Labour* (London: Croom Helm).

Goldie, N. (1988) *I hated it there, but I Miss the People*, Health and Social Services Research Unit, Research Paper 1, September.

Goodman, L. (1987) 'The Approved Social Worker' in Brenton, M. and Ungerson, C. (eds), *Yearbook of Social Policy* (London: Longman).

Gostin, L. (1983) 'The Ideology of Entitlement, in Bean, P. T. (ed.), *Mental Illness: Changes and Trends* (New York: Wiley).

Gruenber, E. and Archer, J. (1979) 'Abandonment of Responsibility for the Seriously Mentally Ill', *Millbank Memorial Fund Quarterly*, vol. 57, pp. 485–506.

Gunn, J. (1977) 'Management of the Mentally Abnormal Offender: Integrated for Parallels, *Proc. Royal Soc. Medicine*, vol. 70, pp. 877–80.

Gunn, J., Maden, T. and Swinton, M. (1991) *Mentally Disordered Prisoners*, Report of the Home Office.

Hersch, C. (1972) 'Social History, Mental Health and Community Control', *American Psychologist*, 27, pp. 749–54.

Higgins, J. (1981) 'Four Years' Experience of an Interim Secure Unit', *British Medical Journal*, vol. 282, pp. 889–93.

HMSO (1957) Royal Commission on the Law Relating to Mental Illness and Mental Deficiency 1954 (Cmnd 169) (The Percy Commission).

HMSO (1961) *Ministry of Health Special Hospitals: The Emery Report*.

HMSO (1967) Royal Commission on the Penal System (1967) vols 1–4.

HMSO (1973) *Report of the Review of Proceedings for the Discharge and Supervision of Psychiatric Patients Subject to Special Restrictions* (Aarvold Committee), Cmnd 5191, Home Office and DHSS.

HMSO (1974) *Report of the Committee on Mentally Abnormal Offenders* (Interim Report), Cmnd 5698.

HMSO (1975) *Report on the Committee on Mentally Abnormal Offenders* (The Butler Report), Cmnd 6244.

HMSO (1978) *Report of the Royal Commission on Civil Liability and Compensation for Personal Injury*, Cmnd 7054, vol. 1 (see paras 246–63) (Pearson Commission).

HMSO (1981) *The Prison Service 4th Report*.

HMSO (1983a) *Mental Health Act 1983* (London: HMSO).

HMSO (1983b) *Memorandum of Parts I to VI, VIII and X of the Mental Health Act 1983*.

HMSO (1984) House of Commons Select Committee Report of Community Care.

HMSO (1985) *The Mental Health Act Commission: First Biennial Report*.

HMSO (1985a) House of Commons, Second Report from the Social Services Committee, Session 1984–1985: *Community Care*, vol. 1.

HMSO (1986b) *Audit Commission Report: Making a Reality of Community Care* (London: HMSO).

HMSO (1987) *Mental Health Act 1983: Memorandum on Parts I to VI and X* (London: HMSO).

HMSO (1987b) National Audit Office. *Community Care Developments*. A Report by the Controller and Auditor General 26 October (London: HMSO)

HMSO (1987) Report of the Interdepartmental Working Group of the Home Office.

HMSO (1988) *Community Care: Agenda for Action* Report to the Secretary of State for Social Services (Sir Roy Griffiths) (London: HMSO).

HMSO (1988) Special Hospital Patients Statistics DH Table 3A.

HMSO (1988) Committee of Inquiry into the Death of Isabel Schwarz (Spokes Enquiry).

HMSO (1988) Report of the Interdepartmental Working Group of the Home Office.

HMSO (1990) Mental Health Act Commission 'Code of Practice'.

Holmes, B. and Johnson, A. (1988) *Cold Comforts: The Scandal of Private Rest Homes* (London: Souvenir Press).

Home Office (1987) Interdepartmental Working Group of Home Office and DHSS officials on Mentally Disordered Offenders in the Prison System in England and Wales, mimeo.

Hood, R. G. (1966) *Homeless Borstal Boys*, Occasional Paper in Social Administration, no. 18 (London: Bell).

Hoult, T. F. (1969) *Dictionary of Modern Sociology* (Totowa, NJ: Littlefield, Adams).

House of Commons Social Services Committee Session (HCSSC) (1984–5) *Community Care.*

Hume, C. and Pullen, I. (1986) *Rehabilitation in Psychiatry* (Edinburgh: Churchill).

Ingleby, D. (1983) 'Mental Health and Social Order', in Cohen, S. and Scull, A. (eds), *Social Control and the State* (Oxford: Blackwell).

Johnson, M. (1988) 'A Throng at Twilight', *The Guardian*, Tuesday 6 December.

Jones, K. (1983) 'Seminars for the Mentally Ill: The Death of a Concept', in Bean, P. T. and Macpherson, S. (eds), *Approaches to Welfare* (London: Routledge & Kegan Paul).

Jones, K. (1985) *After Hospital: A Study of Long-term Psychiatric Patients in York* (Dept of Social Policy and Social Work: York University).

Jones, M. A. (1989) *Textbook on Torts* (2nd edn) (London: Blackstone Press).

Jones, R. M. (1983) *The Mental Health Act 1983* (London: Sweet & Maxwell).

Johnstone, M. (1978) 'The Work of Clinical Psychologist in Primary Care', *Journal of the Royal College of General Practitioners*, 28, pp. 661–9.

Kay, A. and Legg, C. (1986) 'Discharged to the Community: A Review of Housing and Support in London for people leaving Psychiatric Care (London: Good Practices in Mental Health).

Kirk, S. A. and Therrien, M. E. (1975) 'Community Mental Health Myths and the Fate of Former Hospitalised Patients', *Psychiatry*, 38, pp. 209–17.

Klein, J. I. and Glover, S. I. (1983) 'Psychiatric Malpractice', *International Journal of Law and Psychiatry*, vol. 6, no. 2, pp. 131–57.

Laing, W. and Buisson, P. (1985) *Care of Elderly people: The Market for Residential and Nursing homes in Britain* (London).

Lancashire Record Office, Quarter Sessions, Records QS40/3 f.44V.

Lavender, A. and Holloway, F. (eds) (1988) *Community Care in Practice: Services for the Continuing Care Client* (New York: Wiley).

Law Reports (1986) *Queen's Bench Division Regina* v. *Hallstrom and Another*, ex parte; *W Regina* v. *Gardner and Another*, ex parte, L pp. 1090–113.

Mayer, J. A. (1983) 'Notes Towards a Working Definition of Social Control in Historical Analysis', in Cohen, S. and Scull, A. (eds), *Social Control and the State* (Oxford: Blackwell).

Mechanic, D. (1975) *Social Factors affecting Psychotic Behaviour* (Centre for medical sociology and health services research. Research and Analyistic Report series no. 9–75, Madison, Wis.: University of Wisconsin).

Mental Health Act Commission (1985) *The First Biennial Report of the Mental Health Act Commission 1983–1985*, October, 22nd 1985 HC 586.

Mental Health Act Commission (1986) 'Compulsory Treatment in the Community: A Discussion Paper', mimeo.

McLean, C. (1988) *Hospital Discharge Survey* (Essex County Council Social Services).

MIND (1987) 'Compulsory Treatment in the Community', MIND policy paper, mimeo.

Miller, R. D. (1985) 'Commitment to Out-patient Treatment: A National Survey', *Hospital and Community Psychiatry*, March, vol. 36, no. 3, pp. 265–7.

Miller, R. D. (1988a) 'Out-patients and Commitment of the Mentally Ill: An Overview and an Update', *Behavioural Sciences and the Law*, vol. 6, no. 1, pp. 99–118.

Miller, R. D. (1988b) *'Task Force Report on Involuntary Out-patient Treatment'* (American Psychiatric Press).

Mounser, P. and Bean, P. T. (1990) 'Homelessness and the Mentally Disordered, in Oc, T. and Trench, S. (eds); *Current Issues in Planning* (London: Gower).

Mountney, G., Fryers, T. and Freeman, H. L. (1969) 'Psychiatric Emergencies in an Urban Borough', *British Medical Journal*, 1, pp. 478–500.

Myers, J. K. and Bean, L. L. (1968) *A Decade Later: A Follow Up of Social Class and Mental Illness* (New York: Wiley).

National Centre of Health Statistics (1975) *Research in the Service of Mental Health* no. 75–237 (Rockville, MD: DHEW Publications).

New York Times, 8 April 1975 – editorial.

Nottingham Psychiatric Case Register (1987) Bulletin No. 2, June 1987 in mimeo.

Nottingham Psychiatric Case Register (1987): Bulletin No. 3, September 1987 in mimeo.

Okin, R. L. (1984) 'How Community Mental Health Centres are Coping', *Hospital and Community Psychiatry*, 35, pp. 118–25.

Orr, J. H. (1978) 'The Imprisonment of Mentally Abnormal Offenders', *British Journal of Psychiatry*, vol. 133, pp. 194–9.

Parliamentary Debates, Lords Col. 761, 25 January 1982.

Parliamentary Debates (17 January 1986): House of Commons, Cols 1346 to 1350.

Parliamentary Debates (17 June 1986) vol. 89.

Parliamentary Debates (4 December 1985) vol. 88 cols 308–9.

Peay, J. (1988) *Tribunals on Trial: A Study of Decision Making under the Mental Health Act 1983* (Oxford: Clarendon Press).

Posser, W. (1971) *Handbook of the Law of Torts*.

Reid, H. and Wiseman, A. (1986) *When Talking has to Stop* (London: MIND).

Rogers, A. and Faulkner, A. (1987) *A Place of Safety: MIND's Research into Police Referrals to the Psychiatric Services* (London: MIND).

Rose, N. (1986) 'Unreasonable Rights: Mental Illness and the Limits of the Law', *Journal of Law and Society*, vol. 12, no. 2.

Royal College of Psychiatrists (1987) *Community Treatment Orders*, April and October 1987.

Royal College of Psychiatrists (1983) *The Future of the Special Hospitals*.

Royal College of Psychiatrists (1989) *Good Medical Practice in the Aftercare of Potentially Violent or Vulnerable Patients Discharged from Inpatient Psychiatric Treatment*.

Sands, R. G. (1984) 'Correlates of Success and Lack of Success in Deinstitutionalisation' *Community Mental Health Journal*, vol. 120, pp. 223–35.

Saunders, D. H. (1974) 'Optimal Residential Care: First Faculty Presentation', in Horizon House Institute for Research and Development, *Creating the Community Alternative: Options and Innovations*, Proceedings of a Statewide Conference, 19–20 March (Hershey, Pennsylvania).

Sayce, L. (1987) 'Revolution under Review', *Health Service Journal*, 26 November, pp. 1378–9.

Sayer, P. (1988) *The Comforts of Madness* (London: Sceptre books).

Schwartz, D. (1971) 'A Non-Hospital in a Hospital', *American Journal of Public Health*, 61; pp. 2367–82.

Scott, P. D. (1970) 'Punishment or Treatment: Prisons or Hospital', *British Medical Journal*, 18 April, pp. 167–9.

Scott-Moncrieff, L. (1988) 'Comments on the Discussion Document of the Royal College of Psychiatrists regarding Community Treatment Orders', *Bulletin of the Royal College of Psychiatrists*, vol. 12 (June), pp. 22–3.

Scull, A. T. (1977) *Decarceration: Community Treatment and the Deviant, a Radical View* (Englewood Cliff, NJ: Prentice-Hall).

Scull, A. T. (1979) *Museums of Madness: The Social Organisation of Insanity in Nineteenth-Century England* (Harmondsworth: Penguin).

Scull, A. T. (1982) 'Community Corrections: Panacea, Progress or Pretence?', in Abel, R. L. *The Politics of Informal Justice* (ed.), *vol. 1 The American Experience* (New York: Academic Press).

Scull, A. T. (1983) 'The Asylum as Community or the Community as Asylum: Paradoxes and Contradictions of Mental Health Care', in Bean, P. T. (ed.), *Mental Illness: Changes and Trends* (London: Wiley).

Scull, A. T. (1985) 'Deinstitutionalisation and Public Policy', *Social Science and Medicine* vol. 20, no. 5, pp. 545–52.

Sedgwick, P. (1982) *Psycho-Politics* (London: Pluto Press).

Shepherd, M. (1974) 'Mental Illness and the British National Health Service' *American Science of Public Health*, 64(3), pp. 230–32.

Shepherd, M. *et al.* (1966) *Psychiatric Illness in General Practice* (Oxford University Press).

Shepherd, M., Harwin, B. G., Delpla, C. and Cairns, V. (1979) 'Social Work and the Primary Care of Mental Disorder', *Psychological Medicine*, 9, pp. 661–9.

Sims, A. and Symmonds, R. L. (1975) 'Psychiatric Referrals from the Police', *British Journal of Psychiatry*, 127, pp. 171–8.

Slovenko, R. and Luby, E. D. (1974) 'From Moral Treatment to Railroading Out of the Mental Hospital', *Bulletin of the American Academy of Psychiatry and the Law*, December, pp. 223–36.

Smith, J. (1984) *Prison Health Care* (London: British Medical Association).

Snowden, P. (1986) 'Forensic Psychiatry service and RSUs in England and Wales: An Overview', *Criminal Law Review* pp. 789–99.

Talbott, J. A. (1974) 'Stopping the Revolving Door – a Study of Readmissions to a State Hospital, *Psychiatric Quarterly*, 48, pp. 159–68.

Task Force (1987) *Involuntary Commitment to Out-patient Treatment*, American Psychiatric Association, Task Force Report No. 26.

Tenant, C., Bebbington, P. and Hurray, J. (1981) 'The Short Term Outcome of Neurotic Disorders in the Community: The Relation of Remission to Clinical Factors and to "Neutralising" Life Events', *British Journal of Psychiatry*, 139, pp. 213–20.

Tower Hamlets Mental Health and Housing Working Party (1986) *Stepping Out: Mental Health, Housing and Community Care in Tower Hamlets: A Report by the Tower Hamlets Mental Health and Housing Working Party* (November).

United States Senate Subcommittee on Long Term Care (1975) *The Role of Nursing Homes in Caring for Discharged Mental Patients (and the Birth of a For-profit Boarding Home Industry)*. Supporting Paper No. 7 of series 'Nursing Home Care in the United States: Failure in Public Policy' (Washington, DC: Government Printing Office).

Verdun-Jones, S. (1989) 'Sentencing the Partly Mad and the Partly Bad: The Case of the Hospital Order in England and Wales', *International Journal of Law and Psychiatry*, vol. 12, no. 1, pp. 1–28.

Walker, N. and McCabe, S. (1973) *Crime and Insanity in England*, vols I and II (Edinburgh University Press).

Washbrook, R. (1977) 'The Psychiatrically Ill Prisoner', *The Lancet* 18 June, pp. 1302–3.

Wells, J. (1985) *Life after Harwood Road: A Follow-up Study of Former Residents of Harwood Hostel and Recommendations for Service Development.* (London Borough of Hammersmith and Fulham Social Services Department).

Wing, J. (1975) 'Planning and Evaluating Services for Chronically Handicapped Psychiatric Patients in the UK,' presented at the Conference on Alternatives to Mental Hospital Treatment (University of Wisconsin, Madison, October).

Wolpert, J. (1975) 'Service Facility Representation in Urban Communities', (Princeton, NJ: School of Architecture and Urban Planning, mimeo).

Wolpert, J., Dear, M. and Crawford, R. (1974) 'Mental Health Satellite Facilities in the Community', Presented at the National Institute of Mental Health, Centre for Studies of Metropolitan Problems Seminar Series, Rockville, Md., 24 Jan.

World Health Organisation (1973) *Psychiatry and Primary Medical Care* (Copenhagen: WHO Regional Office for Europe).

Index